# ENJOY CHINESE CUISINE

Co-Published by Japan Publications Trading Co., Ltd and Joie, Inc.


**Distributors:**
**UNITED STATES:** Kodansha America, Inc., through Oxford University Press, 198 Madison Avenue, New York, NY 10016
**CANADA:** Fitzhenry & Whiteside Ltd., 195 Allstate Parkway, Markham, Ontario L3R 4T8
**AUSTRALIA AND NEW ZEALAND:** Bookwise International, 174 Cormack Road, Wingfield, SA 5013 Australia
**ASIA AND OTHER COUNTRIES:** Japan Publications Trading Co., Ltd., 1-2-1, Sarugaku-cho, Chiyoda-ku, Tokyo, 101-0064 Japan

Original Copyright ©2003 by Judy Lew
4th Printing September 2007
World rights reserved Published by JOIE, INC. 1-8-3, Hirakawa-cho, Chiyoda-ku, Tokyo 102-0093 Japan
No Part of this book or portions thereof may be reproduced in any form or by any means including electronic retrieval systems without prior written approval from the author or publisher.
Printed in Japan


ISBN 13 : 978-4-88996-126-3
ISBN 10 : 4-88996-126-7

# FOREWORD

The title of this book expresses the intent and purpose for which it was written. You will find that the key to great Chinese cooking lies in learning to enjoy yourself foremost and letting everything else follow.

This book will guide you through the simple techniques necessary for preparing the basic ingredients contained in the easy-to-follow recipes. The recipes have been developed and tested in Chinese cooking classes, along with a few personal favorites that have been handed down from family generations. Suggestions for meal planning have been reduced to a simple chart, for quick and easy reference.

The highly nutritious ingredients and quick sealing cooking methods of Chinese cooking are consistent with the emergence of a health and diet oriented society. The informal Chinese dinner is especially suited for today's life styles. Nutritious, economical and easy to prepare, Chinese food also happens to be very delicious. Thus, this book's emphasis has been placed upon the preparation of dishes used in everyday Chinese meals.

As you gain proficiency and personal confidence in Chinese cooking you will find this book helpful in adapting various recipes to your own personal tastes and experimenting with different ingredients to achieve a desired result. I encourage all my students and readers to go beyond the recipes, substitute ingredients, and—most importantly—have fun and Enjoy Chinese Cooking.

*Judy Lew*

# ACKNOWLEDGMENT

To my loving parents Hing Ng and Po Kim Ng. For Willkie, Kim and Pam to enjoy.

The successful production of this book involved the hard work and cooperation of many people, to all these people my sincere thanks for all of your constant encouragement and assistance.
The expert creative work of my chief editor Mr. Naito and the intuitive and language abilities of Ms. Nagasawa is very much appreciated. Without their direct assistance the book would not be a reality.
To my publisher, Mr. Shiro Shimura and everyone at JOIE, INC. my most warm thank you that I should come to be associated with this most generous and professional company.
To Ms. Kane Yamanaka thank you for your valuable guidance. To Shuichi thank you always for your inspirational talents.
To my friend and professional photographer Mr. George Nakauye, thank you for your skill as an artist and photographer and your time and patience while you waited for each recipe. Most of all thank you for your expertise in assisting in the layout of each photograph.
Special thanks to Mr. Tomio Moriguchi for your constant support in all of my ventures.
To Mr. Paul Ng as always thank you for your wisdom.
My sincere gratitude to Mr. Ronald Lee for your generous assistance in the Chinese translation.
I leave to the end to thank my friend and fellow colleague Ms. Yukiko Moriyama Trunnell for the expert translation of my book into Japanese.
Thank you for your patience, belief in my work and for keeping the faith that I could do it and now I am definitely sure that this whole project is totally worthwhile and owed to you. To Yukiko... thank you always.

# BASIC TIPS

These basic tips will save you time and make for the successful preparation of a Chinese meal.

1. Thoroughly read the INFORMATION pages of this book, paying special attention to the **Cornstarch for Thickening** portion appearing in the **Stir-Frying** section. Become acquainted with the techniques of cooking and the various equipment available to accomplish this purpose. Always read the entire recipe before you attempt to cook.

2. Organize in advance what you need to do. Decide which dishes can be kept warm and cook those courses first. Have all the required ingredients cut and measured for each dish and arranged on a tray such that everything will be on hand.

3. Slicing meat against the grain of the long muscle fibers will result in added tenderness when the meat is cooked. Partially frozen meat is easier to slice and more uniform slices can be obtained.

4. The use of garlic enhances the flavor of cooked food. With the wide blade of the cleaver, gently hit the clove of garlic, separating the skin which should be removed and discarded. Then crush the garlic with the blade of the cleaver. Crushed garlic may be added to most any dish. Just add the crushed garlic to oil heating in the wok. After the flavor has been released, the garlic may be removed or left in the wok while cooking the rest of the ingredients. Be careful not to burn the garlic.

5. Shaohsing wine and other rice wines may be replaced with dry sherry in most recipes. Recipes calling for *mirin*, a Japanese sweet rice wine, should not be replaced with Chinese rice wine. Chinese rice wine and *mirin* are not directly interchangeable.

6. Chicken stock may be used in place of water in recipes other than pastries, doughs, or sweet and sour dishes. This will result in a richer flavor. Canned chicken broth is a good substitute if you do not have time to make your own.

7. Dried forest mushrooms and other dried foods must be soaked in warm water before using in the recipe. They should be soaked until soft, removed, and then rinsed. The usual size of a medium mushroom after soaking is approximately three inches in diameter.

8. The recipes contained in this book were tested and developed using **Japanese** soy sauce which is considered a medium soy sauce. Use a medium soy sauce unless otherwise specified for best results.

9. A recipe requiring prawns will necessitate the proper shelling and deveining of the prawns. This is done by first removing the transparent shell. Cut open the top of the prawn to expose the black sandy vein. Remove the vein by gently pulling it out. The blue vein underneath the prawn should be left alone. Rinse the prawns and towel dry. Proceed with the recipe.

10. Always use your judgment in the substitution of ingredients called for in a recipe. Most ingredients used in this book are explained in the glossary. Be creative and do not be afraid to adapt the recipes to your own personal tastes.

T = tablespoon      t = teaspoon      C = cup

# CONTENTS

# METRIC TABLES

## Liquid Measures

| U.S. Customary system | oz. | g. | ml. |
|---|---|---|---|
| $^1/_{16}$ cup = 1 T. | $^1/_2$ oz. | 14 g. | 15 ml. |
| $^1/_4$ cup = 4 T. | 2 oz. | 60 g. | 59 ml. |
| $^1/_2$ cup = 8 T. | 4 oz. | 115 g. | 118 ml. |
| 1 cup = 16 T. | 8 oz. | 225 g. | 236 ml. |
| 1$^3/_4$ cup | 14 oz. | 400 g. | 414 ml. |
| 2 cups = 1 pint | 16 oz. | 450 g. | 473 ml. |
| 3 cups | 24 oz. | 685 g. | 710 ml. |
| 4 cups | 32 oz. | 900 g. | 946 ml. |

General points of information that may prove valuable or of interest:

1 British fluid ounce = 28.5 ml.
1 American fluid ounce = 29.5 ml.

1 Japanese cup = 200 ml.
1 British cup = 200 ml. = 7 British fl oz.
1 American cup = 240 ml. = 8 American fl oz.

1 British pint = 570 ml. = 20 British fl oz.
1 American pint = 470 ml. = 16 American fl oz.
T. = tablespoon  oz. = ounce  g. = gram  ml. = milliliter

## Weights

| grams to ounces | ounces to grams* |
|---|---|
| 1 g. = 0.035 oz. | $^1/_4$ oz. = 7 g. |
| 5 g. = $^1/_6$ oz. | $^1/_2$ oz. = 14 g. |
| 10 g. = $^1/_3$ oz. | 1 oz. = 30 g. |
| 28 g. ≑ 1 oz. | 2 oz. = 60 g. |
| 100 g. = 3$^1/_2$ oz. | 4 oz. = 115 g. |
| 200 g. = 7 oz. | 6 oz. = 170 g. |
| 500 g. = 18 oz. | 8 oz. = 225 g. |
| 1000 g. = 35 oz. | 16 oz. = 450 g. |

grams × 0.035 = ounces
ounces × 28.35 = grams

*Equivalent

## Linear Measures

| inches to centimeters | centimeters to inches* |
|---|---|
| $^1/_2$ in. = 1.27 cm. | 1 cm. = $^3/_8$ in. |
| 1 in. = 2.54 cm. | 2 cm. = $^3/_4$ in. |
| 2 in. = 5.08 cm. | 3 cm. = 1$^1/_6$ in. |
| 4 in. = 10.16 cm. | 4 cm. = 1$^1/_2$ in. |
| 5 in. = 12.7 cm. | 5 cm. = 2 in. |
| 10 in. = 25.4 cm. | 10 cm. = 4 in. |
| 15 in. = 38.1 cm. | 15 cm. = 5$^3/_4$ in. |
| 20 in. = 50.8 cm. | 20 cm. = 8 in. |

inches × 2.54 = centimeters
centimeters × 0.39 = inches

in. = inch   cm. = centimeter

## Temperature

| Fahrenheit (F.) to Celsius (C.) | | Celsius (C.) to Fahrenheit (F.) | |
|---|---|---|---|
| freezer storage | −10F. = −23.3C. | freezer storage | −20C. = −4F. |
| | 0F. = −17.7C. | | −10C. = 14F. |
| water freezes | 32F. = 0 C. | water freezes | 0C. = 32F. |
| | 68F. = 20 C. | | 10C. = 50F. |
| | 100F. = 37.7C. | | 50C. = 122F. |
| water boils | 212F. = 100 C. | water boils | 100C. = 212F. |
| | 300F. = 148.8C. | | 150C. = 302F. |
| | 400F. = 204.4C. | | 200C. = 392F. |

The water boiling temperature given is at sea level.

Conversion factors:
C. = F. − 32 × $^5/_9$
$$F. = \frac{C. \times 9}{5} + 32$$

C. = Celsius   F. = Fahrenheit

# Dim Sum and Appetizers

"Dim Sum," literally translated, is dot of the heart, but more appropriately should be termed heart's delight.

A dim sum luncheon consists of bite-size meat and vegetable morsels which are steamed, pan fried, deep fried or baked, and served with tea. These small pieces of food can be enhanced by dipping in a selection of sauces, such as hot sauce, soy sauce, hot mustard, or vinegar dips.

Most restaurants usually serve dim sum between the hours of 11:00 A.M. to 3:00 P.M. Carts filled with the appetizers are constantly circulated throughout the restaurant. Stop the waitress and make your selections. After the meal, the small plates are counted and totalled. Eat slowly and enjoy!

Any combination of vegetables can be adapted to this recipe.

## INGREDIENTS: makes 50 won tons

| | |
|---|---|
| 1 lb (450 g) | Won Ton wrappers |
| **Filling** | |
| 1/2 lb (225 g) | ground pork |
| 1/4 C | chopped onions |
| 1 | Chinese sausage, chopped |
| 1/2 C | chopped bamboo shoots |
| 1/2 C | chopped green onions |
| 1 t | *mirin* or rice wine |
| 1 t | salt |
| 1 t | soy sauce |
| 2 t | cornstarch |
| | |
| 1 | egg white |
| 3 C | oil for deep-frying (375°F, 190°C) |

Some SWEET AND SOUR SAUCE (pg.11)

\* Fry ahead and reheat in oven (375°F, 190°C 5 min).

1. Combine filling ingredients.

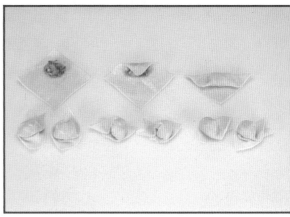

2. Place 1 t filling (heaping) on the top corner of wrapper. Fold tip of wrapper over the meat. Roll wrapper until halfway down covering meat. Put a small dab of egg on the left hand side of covered meatball. Pull sides back and pinch together, placing one side on top of the egg white.

3. Fry in oil for 2 min. until golden brown, turning occasionally. Serve with Sweet and Sour Sauce.

**PRESENTATION**

## 甜酸醬 SWEET AND SOUR SAUCE

**INGREDIENTS:** makes 1¹/₂ C

³/₄ C   water
1¹/₂ T   cornstarch
2 T   rice vinegar
3 T   catsup
²/₃ C   sugar
Dash soy sauce

∗ Mix sauce together ahead. Bring to full boil just before serving Sauce can be kept warm or reheated.

Mix together all ingredients in order. Cook and stir until sauce comes to a full boil. Pour into bowl to use with appetizers.

**Serve as a side dish with Chow Mein or FRIED RICE (p. 38).**

## INGREDIENTS: makes 10-12 rolls

**Egg roll skins (10-12 skins)**
| | |
|---|---|
| 2 T | cornstarch dissolved in 1/4 C water |
| 4 | eggs |
| 1/2 t | salt |
| Some | oil |

**Egg roll filling**
| | |
|---|---|
| 1 C | lean pork sliced thin |
| 2 T | oil |
| 1/2 C | chopped onions |
| 1 C | beansprouts |
| 1/2 C | chopped celery |
| 1/4 C | chopped bamboo shoots |
| 2 T | chopped water chestnuts |
| 2 | large forest mushrooms, sliced (soaked until soft and rinsed) |
| 1/2 t | salt or to taste |
| 1 T | oyster sauce |
| 1/2 C | water or soup stock |
| Some | cornstarch for thickening |

**Batter**
| | |
|---|---|
| 1/2 C | flour |
| 1/4 C | cornstarch |
| 1 t | baking powder |
| 1/2 t | baking soda |
| 3/4 C | cold water |
| | |
| 3 C | oil for deep-frying (375°F, 190°C) |

\* If store bought wrappers must be used, try to use the thinnest wrappers available. Store bought egg roll wrappers need not be dipped into batter before deep-frying.

1. Combine cornstarch mixture, eggs and salt. Beat until well blended. Pour a small amount of oil into an 8 in (20 cm) teflon or non-sticky frying pan. Rub oil in with a paper towel. Reserve paper towel. Heat skillet on medium heat until hot.

2. Pour small amount of egg mixture into skillet and coat bottom of pan with egg mixture. Quickly pour excess out, back into bowl. Cook until edge pulls from sides of pan. Remove from the pan and set aside. Continue until all of egg mixture is used, oiling the skillet as needed.

3. Heat oil in wok until hot. Add pork and cook until all pink is gone (2 min.)

4. Add all other ingredients except cornstarch.

5. Cover, bring to boil, cook ½ min.

6. Thicken with cornstarch and water to form a fairly thick sauce. Set aside and allow to cool. Refrigerate until ready to use.

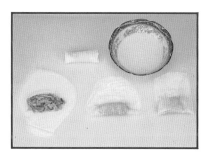

7. Place about 3 T filling on the lower bottom of round wrapper. If using square wrappers, place like a diamond in front of you. Bring bottom up to cover filling and roll once. Fold sides in to overlap. Place a small amount of batter at top of wrapper to seal. Continue to roll wrapper until closed. (If no batter is available, mix small amount of flour with water to use as seal.) Mix together batter.

## PRESENTATION

8. Heat 3C oil in wok to 375°F (190°C). Dip each egg roll into batter and deep-fry in oil for 2 min. or until golden brown. Turn egg rolls as soon as possible to keep top from breaking open. Continue turning to fry evenly. Continue to fry remaining egg rolls in the same manner. If oil gets too hot, turn to medium high. Always try to maintain 375°F (190°C.)

Serve with other appetizers as part of dim sum lunch.

# INGREDIENTS: 3-4 servings

### Filling

| | |
|---|---|
| 3/4 lb (340 g) | shrimp shelled, deveined and chopped |
| 1/4 C | bamboo shoots chopped |
| 1 t | salt |
| 1 t | sesame seed oil |
| 1/2 t | sugar |
| 1 | egg white |
| 2 T | cornstarch |

Combine filling ingredients and set in refrigerator for one hour.

### Dough

| | |
|---|---|
| 1 C | wheat starch |
| 1/2 C | tapioca starch |
| 1/2 t | salt |
| 1 C | boiling water |
| 2 T | oil |

✻ Dough can be made ahead. Wrap with foil or plastic wrap. Dough keeps one day at room temperature.

1. Mix wheat starch, tapioca starch and salt together in a large pot. Make a well in center and pour in boiling water.

2. Stir to moisten ingredients.

3. Cover pot and allow to rest 10 min.

4. Knead until a smooth dough forms adding oil. Set aside. Keep covered until ready to use.

5. Roll portions of dough into a long roll and cut walnut size pieces. Roll each piece in hand until smooth. Then generously oil cleaver and counter top. Press out dough to form a 3 in (8 cm) circle. (Or use a tortilla press.)

6. Pleat half of circle to form a pouch. Put in 2 t filling, cover and pinch ends together.

7. Gently curve dumpling to form a crescent.

8. Place on an oiled steaming plate and steam 15 min.

**PRESENTATION**

Pot stickers are delicious served over a stir-fried vegetable dish such as bok choy or pea pods.

## INGREDIENTS: makes 40-50

| | | | | |
|---|---|---|---|---|
| ¹/₂ pkg | Siu Mai wrappers (8 oz, 225 g pkg contains about 80 wrappers). | | ¹/₂ t | sugar |
| | | | 2 T | cornstarch |
| **Filling** | | | | |
| 1 lb (450 g) | ground pork | | 3 C | oil for frying |
| 2 C | chopped nappa | | | |
| ¹/₄ C | chopped onions | | 3 C | chicken soup stock |
| 1 T | chopped ginger root | | | |
| 1 t | soy sauce | | | |
| 1 t | salt | | | |
| 2 t | sesame seed oil | | | |
| 1 t | wine | | | |

\* Filling may be prepared ahead and refrigerated. Fill pot stickers, brown them and then they can be frozen. To reheat, allow to defrost, refry for one minute and continue with the recipe.

1. Combine filling ingredients.

2. Place 2 t filling in center of wrapper, wet edge and seal to form a half circle.

3. Hold top edge and press down to flatten bottom.

4. Heat a 12 in (30 cm) skillet with small amount of oil and fry pot stickers on medium high heat until brown on all sides.

5. Pour ½ C soup stock, cover and cook until liquid is absorbed. Serve with soy sauce or vinegar dip, or hot sesame seed oil.

**PRESENTATION**

Use other filling ingredients such as Chinese sausages or sweet bean paste.

## INGREDIENTS: makes 16 buns

**Filling**

| | |
|---|---|
| 1/2 T | oil |
| 1/4 C | diced onions |
| 1/2 | large forest mushroom (soaked, rinsed and diced) |
| 1 T | hoisin sauce |
| 1 T | catsup |
| 3/4 T | sugar |
| 1/2 T | oyster sauce |
| 1/8 t | garlic powder |
| 1/4 t | salt |
| 1/4 C | water |
| 1/2 T | cornstarch dissolved in 1 T water |
| 3/4 C | diced cooked barbecued pork |

**Dough**

| | |
|---|---|
| 1/2 C | warm water |
| 1 T | sugar |
| 2 T | dry yeast |
| 3/4 C | warm milk |
| 1/2 C | sugar |
| 3-3 1/2 C | all purpose flour |
| 1/2 t | salt |
| | |
| 16 | pieces waxed paper (3 × 3 in, 8 × 8 cm) |

\* Filling may be made ahead. Freeze unused portion.

1. Add oil to wok, cook onions and mushrooms on high heat for 1/2 min.

2. Add all other ingredients, except cornstarch and barbecued pork. Allow to cook 1/2 min.

3. Thicken with cornstarch mixture to form a thick sauce. Mix in diced pork cool.

18

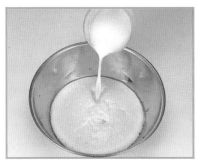

4. In a large bowl, dissolve 1T sugar and yeast in warm water. Allow mixture to sit 5 min.

5. Combine warm milk with ½C sugar, stir to dissolve sugar. Add to yeast mixture.

6. Combine 3C of flour with the salt. Stir into liquid yeast mixture.

7. Stir until a firm dough is formed. Turn out on floured surface and knead until smooth, adding extra flour if necessary (about 10 min.).

8. Place in a greased bowl, turn dough over and cover with a towel. Allow to rise until doubled in bulk.

9. Dough is doubled in volume.

10. Punch down dough, knead 2 min. and allow dough to rest 2 min. Cut into 16 equal pieces.

11. Roll each piece into a ball, then roll into a 4in (10cm) circle, dusting with flour if necessary. Allow dough to rest 2 min. Roll out other pieces while waiting. Place 1T filling (heaping) in center of dough.

12. Pull dough over filling and close top by pleating, pinching and twisting edges together.

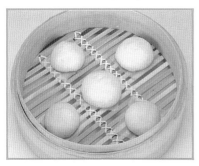

**PRESENTATION**

13. Place on a piece of waxed paper, pleated edge down. Space 2 in (5 cm) apart on a steaming plate. Allow to rise 45 min in a warm oven (95°F, 35°C).

14. Steam in wok for 15 min at full steam. Remove cover carefully so water will not drop on top of buns.

# 叉燒烤包 **BAKED BARBECUED PORK BUNS**

Use the same filling as STEAMED BARBECUED PORK BUNS (p. 18).

## INGREDIENTS: makes 16 buns

| | | | |
|---|---|---|---|
| 2 T | dry yeast | 1 | egg white beaten |
| $1/4$ C | warm water | | with 2 t water |
| | (110°F, 43°C) | | |
| 1 T | sugar | 2 T | melted butter |
| | | | |
| $1/2$ C | warm milk | 16 | pieces waxed |
| $1/4$ C | melted butter or | | paper (3 × 3 in, |
| | margarine | | 8 × 8 cm) |
| $1/2$ C | sugar | | |
| 1 t | salt | 7 oz (200 g) | barbecued pork |
| 2 | large eggs (room | | filling (pg. 18·19) |
| | temp.) | | |
| | | | |
| 3-3$1/2$ C | all purpose flour | | |
| | (or use high pro- | | |
| | tein flour) | | |

\* Freeze or keep refrigerated until needed. To serve, reheat in a 325°F (163°C) oven for about 10 min and brush again with melted butter.

1. In a large bowl, dissolve yeast in warm water and stir in 1 T sugar. Allow mixture to sit 10 min.

2. Combine warm milk, melted butter, sugar, salt and eggs. Add to yeast mixture and beat together.

3. Add 2 C of the flour to make a thick batter, beat until smooth. Gradually mix in enough of the remaining flour (about 1 C) to make a stiff dough. Turn out onto a floured surface; knead until smooth (about 10 min).

4. Working in remaining ½ C of flour as needed to keep dough from sticking.

5. Place dough in a greased bowl, turn dough over, cover and allow to rise in a warm place until doubled in bulk.

6. Dough has doubled in volume.

7. Punch down dough, knead 2 min and allow dough to rest 2 min. Cut into 16 equal pieces.

8. Roll each piece into a ball, then roll into a 4 in (10 cm) circle, dusting with flour if necessary. Allow dough to rest 2 min. Roll out other pieces while waiting. Place 1 T filling (heaping) in center of dough.

9. Pull dough over filling and close top by pleating, pinching and twisting edge together.

10. Place on piece of waxed paper, pleated edge down. Space 2 in (5 cm) apart on a cookie sheet. Allow to rise 45 min in a warm oven (95°F, 35°C).

11. Brush gently with egg white mixture. Bake at 350°F (175°C) for 15 min or until golden brown. Remove from oven and brush immediately with 2 T melted butter. For a sweeter taste, brush with honey too.

## PRESENTATION

Use as a first course to a Chinese meal.

## INGREDIENTS: 24 rolls

**Filling**
| | |
|---|---|
| 2 | large black forest mushrooms |
| 1 C | chicken breast |
| 1/2 C | bamboo shoots |
| 1/2 C | onions |
| 2 T | oil |
| 2 T | oyster sauce |
| 1/4 t | salt |
| | |
| 8 | sheets phyllo (pg.24) |
| 1/4 C | oil |

1. Soak mushrooms to soften and rinse. Slice chicken, mushrooms, bamboo shoots, and onions into thin strips. Heat oil in wok and cock chicken until meat turns white. Then add mushrooms, bamboo shoots, and onions, cook ½ min.

2. Add oyster sauce and salt. Mix thoroughly and remove. Allow mixture to cool before wrapping.

3. Cut each phyllo sheet into thirds. Take one piece and brush half of sheet with oil, fold in half to form a square. Brush with more oil.

4. Place 1 T filling in lower corner. Fold corner up to cover filling, then roll up once, fold both sides in to overlap, continue rolling up, Brush entire surface with oil.

**PRESENTATION**

5. Place on cookie sheet and bake at 400°F (205°C) for 15 min or until golden brown.

# 咖喱角 CURRY TURNOVERS

## Curry flavored filling goes well with crisp phyllo.

## INGREDIENTS: 24 turnovers

| Filling | | | |
|---|---|---|---|
| 1 T | oil | ¹/₄ t | sugar |
| ¹/₂ lb (225 g) ground beef or pork | | 1 T | catsup |
| ¹/₂ C | chopped onions | 8 | sheets of phyllo pastry 13 × 17in |
| ¹/₂ C | chopped bamboo shoots | | (33 × 43cm) |
| 1-2 t | curry | ¹/₂ C | oil |
| ³/₄ t | salt | | |

✳ Phyllo is a tissue thin Mid-Eastern pastry dough, made of flour, egg and water. Usually comes in 1 pound boxes, containing about 20 sheets rolled up. Check edges to be sure of freshness, should be smooth, not crumbly. To keep from drying during wrapping, spread damp towel on counter. Place a sheet of waxed paper over towel, put phyllo sheets on top, cover with another sheet of waxed paper and damp towel. Make sure phyllo sheets are not directly touching damp towel.

1. Heat 1 T oil in wok, brown meat, drain off excess fat. Add all other ingredients and mix together and cook 2 min. Remove and allow to cool.

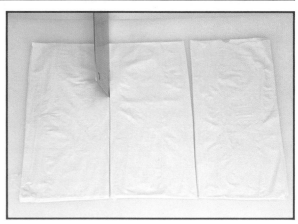

2. Cut phyllo sheets into thirds lengthwise and stack. Keep moist by covering with waxed paper and damp towel.

3. Take one strip, brush half of strip with oil and fold in half lengthwise.

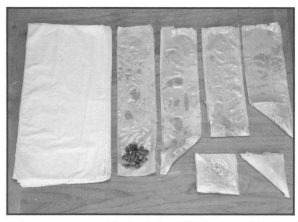

4. Brush top surface with oil and place 1 T filling (heaping) on bottom of strip. Fold strip over filling so bottom of strip meets left side. Continue folding at right angles. Tuck at top to form triangle. Brush top and bottom of triangle with oil. Repeat until all dough and filling is used.

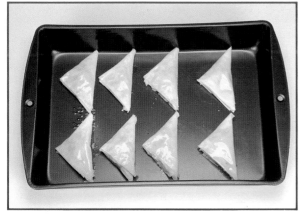

5. Place on cookie sheet and bake at 400°F (205°C) for 15 min or until golden brown. Also may be fried in oil until golden brown.

**PRESENTATION**

## Serve as an appetizer for a buffet or party.

### INGREDIENTS: makes 30 siu mai

| | | | |
|---|---|---|---|
| 30 | Siu Mai wrappers | 2 | large forest mushrooms chopped (soaked and rinsed) |
| **Filling** | | | |
| 1 lb (450 g) | coarse ground pork | | |
| 1 | Chinese sausage chopped | 1½ t | salt |
| 2 T | bamboo shoots chopped | ½ t | sugar |
| 2 T | water chestnuts chopped | 1 t | wine |
| ¼ C | onions chopped | 1 t | sesame seed oil |
| | | 1 t | soy sauce |
| | | 2 T | cornstarch |

1. Combine all filling ingredients.

2. Place 1 T filling in center of wrapper. Gather edge of wrapper around filling. Flatten the bottom, squeeze the center and smooth off the top with wet fingers.

3. Place on steaming plate ½ in (1.5 cm) apart. Steam for 20 min.

**PRESENTATION**

# Soups

The role of soup in a Chinese meal is that of a beverage served throughout the meal, but traditionally towards the end of the meal.

Use as a base for any soup or for any kind of cooking.

### 1. Winter melon soup

½ lb (225 g) winter melon. Remove hard outer skin and seeds. Dice in ½ in (1½ cm) cubes. Add some diced black forest mushrooms for color and flavor. (Soak and rinse mushrooms first). Bring soup stock to a full boil, add all ingredients, cover and cook slowly for 10 min.

### 2. *Tofu* (bean curd) soup

½ lb (225 g) or 1 C *tofu* cut into small squares. Try to add some amount of green vegetable to help the color. Cook gently for 1 min.

\* All of the above soups are prepared basically the same way. Vary the ingredients to vary the soup. Use different garnishes such as cooked ham or crab to make soups more elegant. Soups are usually served with the dinner, but to make serving easier, serve soup before the main dishes.

# BASIC CHICKEN STOCK (from bones or whole chicken)

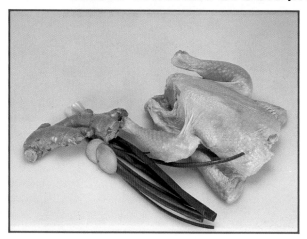

## INGREDIENTS: makes 6C

| | |
|---|---|
| 1 | chicken or 3 C bones |
| 8 C | water |
| 2 | slices ginger root |
| 1 | scallion |

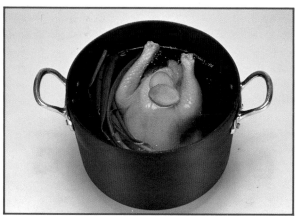

1.  Place the chicken or bones, ginger, scallion and the water in a pot and bring to a full boil on high heat. Skim froth and fat, turn temperature to simmer, cover and simmer stock for 1 hour or until chicken is cooked.

2.  Remove chicken or bones and strain soup stock with a fine mesh strainer. Cheese cloth may be used if desired. Skim soup of excess fat. Allow soup to cool, then refrigerate. Fat will harden on the surface and can be easily removed with a strainer.

**PRESENTATION**

* Salt is usually not added until soup stock is used. Soup stock can be used in place of water in most recipes, making the dish more flavorful. Canned chicken broth is a good substitute.
* Stock may be stored in the refrigerator for up to 5 days. Freeze stock in ice cube trays, then store in plastic bags and use as needed.
* Use pork bones to make pork soup stock or a combination of pork and chicken bones. Increase water and simmering time for larger bones.
* The proper proportion of water to bones is just enough water to cover the bones, if enough bones have been accumulated.
* Use beef stock only for beef dishes.
* A whole chicken can be used instead of bones. After cooking, reserve chicken for another use.

Serve soup with EGG ROLLS (p. 12) or CHICKEN ROLLS (p. 22).

## INGREDIENTS: 6-8 servings as dinner soup

| | |
|---|---|
| 25 | Won Ton wrappers |
| **Filling** | |
| 1/2 C | ground pork (unseasoned) |
| 1/2 C | prawns, shelled and deveined |
| 2 T | water chestnuts |
| 2 T | bamboo shoots |
| 1/2 t | salt |
| 1 t | cornstarch |
| 1 t | rice wine |
| | |
| 1 | egg white to seal wrappers |
| **Soup** | |
| 8-10 C | chicken stock (seasoned with 1 t salt or to taste) |
| 2 | forest mushrooms, (soaked until soft, rinsed and sliced) |
| 1/2 C | sliced bamboo shoots |
| 1/4 C | sliced water chestnuts |
| | |
| 2 C | sliced Chinese greens (bok choy) or any green leafy vegetables |
| 1/4 C | chopped green onions |

1. Chop ground pork, prawns, water chestnuts and bamboo shoots until smooth. Add salt, cornstarch and wine mix until smooth, refrigerate until ready to wrap won tons.

2. Place 1 t filling (heaping) on the top corner of wrapper. Fold tip of wrapper over the meat. Roll wrapper until halfway down covering meat. Put a small dab of egg on the left hand side of covered meatball. Pull sides back and pinch together, placing one side on top of the egg white.

3. Boil won tons in a large pot of boiling water for 2 min.

4. Remove and rinse in cold water, drain. Set aside.

5. Bring chicken stock to a boil, adding salt, bamboo shoots, water chestnuts and mushrooms. Add won tons to soup, bring to a boil, reduce temperature and cook 5 min.

6. Add green vegetables during last minute of cooking. Toss green onions on top to garnish.

∗ Prepare filling ahead and freeze, or freeze after wrapping through step 2. To freeze: Wrap won tons, place on a tray in a single layer, making sure they are not touching. When frozen, remove from tray and place in an air tight freezer container. May keep frozen up to one month. Cook them later straight from a frozen state as though they were just wrapped.

∗ To cut steps down even more, won tons may be prepared through step 3. Then they can either be frozen in small packages of 8 or 10. To use, must allow to defrost and then continue with the recipe. Or prepare through step 3 and keep covered with water in the refrigerator. Use as soon as possible. Remember, this is recommended only if you are entertaining and time is limited.

**Handling of won ton wrappers**

∗ Won ton wrappers are sold fresh or frozen, thick or thin, usually in one pound packages. If frozen, defrost, take out the amount needed and wrap the remainder air tight and may refreeze only one time. Fresh wrappers keep one week in the refrigerator. Always cover wrappers from the air to keep from drying out. The white powder on the wrappers is cornstarch. Always keep the side with more cornstarch on the outside when wrapping, so it will cook out.

**PRESENTATION**

Serve with **CHICKEN WITH ALMONDS (p. 89).**

## INGREDIENTS: 4-6 servings

| | |
|---|---|
| 4 C | chicken stock |
| ½ C | slivered pork |
| ¼ C | slivered bamboo shoots |
| 2 | forest mushrooms (soaked, rinsed and sliced thin) |
| ¼ C | cloud ears (2 T dried) soaked, rinsed and chopped |

| | |
|---|---|
| ½ | cube (1 C) *tofu* sliced into thin strips |
| 2 T | soy sauce |
| ½ t | white pepper or to taste |
| 3 T | rice vinegar |
| 1 | egg, beaten |
| 2 T | cornstarch dissolved in 3 T water |
| ¼ C | green onions chopped |
| 2 T | preserved Szechuan vegetable chopped (optional) |
| 1 t | sesame seed oil |

✱ Soup may be prepared ahead and reheated gently. Be sure to rinse cloud ears well because it is sandy. Preserved Szechuan vegetable comes in cans. It is preserved with salt and chili pepper. Rinse before using.

1. Combine stock, pork, bamboo shoots, mushrooms and cloud ears. Bring to a boil and cook for 5 min, stirring to break up pork.

2. Add *tofu* and cook gently for 1 min. And add soy sauce, white pepper and rice vinegar.

3. Add egg and stir.

4. Add cornstarch and water mixture, stir gently and bring to a slow boil.

5. Add green onions and preserved vegetable. Add sesame seed oil just before serving.

**PRESENTATION**

Serve with SPICY PRAWNS (p. 83) or any spicy dish.

## INGREDIENTS: 6 servings

| | |
|---|---|
| 1 C | chicken breast chopped fine |
| 1 | egg white |
| 1 T | rice wine |
| 1 T | cornstarch |
| | |
| 4 C | chicken stock |
| 1 C | creamed corn |
| 1½ t | salt |
| ½ t | white pepper |
| | |
| 1 | egg, beaten |
| 2 T | cornstarch dissolved in 2 T water |
| | |
| 1 | green onion, chopped |
| ¼ C | chopped ham (optional) |

1. Combine chopped chicken breast, egg white, wine and cornstarch. Set aside.

2. Combine soup stock, creamed corn, salt and white pepper. Bring to a boil, adding chicken mixture. Stir to break up chicken and cook 1 min.

3. Add beaten egg in a thin stream and stir slowly in one direction. Thicken with cornstarch and water mixture.

4. Garnish with green onions and ham.

**PRESENTATION**

Garnish this soup with chopped green onion just before serving.

## INGREDIENTS: 4-6 servings

| | |
|---|---|
| 4 C | water or soup stock |
| 1/2 C | ground pork |
| 1/2 C | chopped prawns (shelled, deveined and cleaned) |
| 4 | water chestnuts |
| 1 t | salt |
| 3 | sheets of dried seaweed (tear into small pieces) |
| 1 | egg |
| 1 | green onion |
| 1 t | sesame seed oil |

\* If prawns are not used, substitute more chopped or ground pork. If unable to find ground pork, use lean pork chops and mince the meat yourself.

**PRESENTATION**

1. Bring water to boil. Add about 1/2 C of boiling water to the ground pork and prawns to break up meat. Add to the boiling water in the pot and stir to break up meat.

2. Add salt, chopped water chestnuts, simmer 5 min. Add seaweed and cook 2 min stir in beaten egg.

3. Add chopped green onions and sesame seed oil just before serving.

36

# Rice and Noodles

The staple course served in any Chinese meal consists of either rice or noodles.

Serve with **SWEET AND SOUR CHICKEN (p. 52).**

## INGREDIENTS: 4 servings

| | |
|---|---|
| 2 | eggs, beaten |
| 3 T | oil |
| 3 | strips bacon cut into 1 in (2½ cm) pieces |
| ½ C | cooked meat diced (pork, chicken, shrimp or ham) |
| 1 | small onion diced |
| 1 C | beans prouts |
| 3 C | cooked long grain rice |
| 2-3 T | soy sauce |
| 1 | green onion chopped |

* Other meats and vegetables may be used to produce a variety of fried rice.
* Chinese sausage can be added to recipe. Cut in small pieces and cook with the bacon.

1. Heat 1 T oil in the wok and scramble eggs. Remove and set aside.

2. Fry bacon in the wok until most of the fat is cooked out.

3. Drain off excess fat and replace with 2 T oil.

4. Add cooked meat, onions and bean sprouts. Stir fry about 1 min.

5. Add rice and soy sauce. Fry until rice is hot, turning temperature down if necessary. Add eggs and mix in with rice. Toss in green onions.

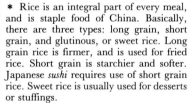

# 白飯 STEAMED WHITE RICE

|  (makes 3 cups) |  (makes 4 cups) |
|---|---|
| 1 C rice (long grain) | 1¹/₂C rice (short grain) |
| 1¹/₂C water | 1³/₄C water |

* Rice is an integral part of every meal, and is staple food of China. Basically, there are three types: long grain, short grain, and glutinous, or sweet rice. Long grain rice is firmer, and is used for fried rice. Short grain is starchier and softer. Japanese *sushi* requires use of short grain rice. Sweet rice is usually used for desserts or stuffings.

* Water proportion changes as more rice is used. If cooking more rice, add enough water to cover rice one inch or water level should be up to first joint of index finger. Increase or decrease water to the firmness desired.

1. Wash rice by rubbing between hands. (Some brands require no washing.)

2. Drain and repeat until water is clear.

3. Add water, cover saucepan and bring to boil.

4. When rice comes to boil, uncover and allow rice to boil until (75%) or most of liquid evaporates and holes form on surface of rice. Cover rice, allow to steam on very low heat for 20 min.

5. Turn heat off and allow rice to sit 5 min on burner. Fluff rice before serving.

**Serve with EGG ROLLS (p. 12).**

## INGREDIENTS: 4 servings

| | |
|---|---|
| 7 oz (200 g) | pan fried noodles |
| 1/4 lb (115 g) | beef, sliced 1/8 in (1/2 cm) thick against the grain |
| 2 t | soy sauce |
| 2 t | cornstarch |
| 1 t | sugar |
| 1 | small onion |
| 1 | small green pepper |
| 1 | tomato |
| 2 T | oil |

**Sauce**

| | |
|---|---|
| 1 C | water |
| 1 T | cornstarch |
| 1/4 C | catsup |
| 1/2 t | salt |
| 2 T | sugar |

\* Add about one teaspoon of curry powder when stir frying the onions and green peppers to make curry beef tomato chow mein.

1. Prepare 7 oz (200 g) pan fried noodles. Set aside.

2. Slice beef.

3. Combine beef slices with soy sauce, cornstarch and sugar.

4. Combine sauce ingredients. Cut onion, green pepper and tomato into wedges.

5. Heat wok and add the oil. Stir-fry the beef until done, remove and set aside.

6. Add onions and peppers to wok, stir-fry a few seconds to break apart onions.

### PRESENTATION

7. Add sauce mixture, bring to full boil to thicken. Add tomato wedges and beef. Stir to combine and mix in noodles.

## 炒麵 PAN FRIED NOODLES

Depending on the type of noodles used, the boiling time will vary. Thin noodles will take less time, about 2 min, while thick noodles will take 6 to 10 min or cook until tender. Follow package instructions if available. Steamed Chinese noodles should be pan fried without boiling first. Use about one half pound of steamed noodles for each recipe of chow mein. Most recipes call for about one half pound of **cooked** noodles.

Some noodles expand more during cooking then others. Use enough dried noodles to get one half pound after cooking.

1. In a large pot, bring some water to a full boil. Cook desired amount of noodles until tender.

2. Remove noodles from pot, rinse with cold water and drain thoroughly.

3. Heat a frying pan (preferably non-stick) on medium high heat. Add about 2T oil and cook noodles in a 1 in (2½ cm) layer until golden brown. Turn noodles over and brown other side, adding more oil if necessary. Remove and set aside.

HOT SPICED CHICKEN (p. 57) is a good combination.

## INGREDIENTS: makes 4 servings

| | |
|---|---|
| 8 oz (225 g) | soft chow mein noodles (steamed Chinese noodles) |
| 3 T | oil |
| | |
| 2 T | oil |
| 1/2 lb (225 g) | pork, sliced thin |
| 1 | small onion, sliced |
| 3 | forest mushrooms (soaked, rinsed and sliced) |
| 1/4 C | sliced water chestnuts |
| 1/4 C | sliced bamboo shoots |
| 1 | stalk celery, sliced |
| 1 C | bean sprouts |
| 1/2 C | pea pods |
| 1 T | *mirin* |
| 1 t | salt |
| 1 C | soup stock |
| | |
| 1 | green onion cut in 1 in (2 1/2 cm) pieces |
| 1 T | cornstarch dissolved in 1 T water |

1. Brown the noodles in 3 T oil on medium high heat, remove and set aside. Add the 2 T oil to wok and cook pork on high heat until no longer pink. (2 min)

2. Add all other ingredients except green onions and cornstarch mixture. Cover and bring to full boil, allow to steam 1 min.

3. Toss in green onions and stir in cornstarch mixture to thicken.

4. Add noodles to vegetable mixture and toss to combine.

## STEAMED CHINESE NOODLE

If unable to obtain soft Chinese noodles, sometimes called steamed Chinese noodles, substitute dried noodels. Dried noodles must be boiled according to package instructions, rinsed and drained, then fry in oil until brown. Pea pods may be substituted; use green pepper, bok choy, or thin sliced carrots. Other meats may be used such as chicken, shrimp, beef, barbecued pork or ham.

## PRESENTATION

Delicious served with BARBECUED SPARERIBS (p. 61).

## INGREDIENTS: 4 servings

| | | | |
|---|---|---|---|
| 7 oz (200 g) | pan fried noodles (pg. 41) | 1/4 C | sliced water chestnuts |
| | | 1/3 C | sliced bamboo shoots |
| 1/2 lb (225 g) | prawns (shelled, deveined and rinsed) | 2 | large forest mushrooms (soaked, rinsed and sliced 1/4 in, 3/4 cm thick) |
| 1/4 lb (115 g) | scallops | 3 T | oil |
| 1/4 t | salt | 1 | clove garlic minced |
| 1 t | wine | 3/4 C | soup stock |
| 1/2 | egg white | 1 T | oyster sauce |
| 1 T | cornstarch | 1/2 t | salt or to taste |
| 1 | small onion, wedged | Some cornstarch and water for thickening | |
| 1/4 lb (115 g) | pea pods | | |
| 1 C | bok choy leaves | | |

＊ Other vegetables may be used. Use 12 oz (340 g) chicken instead of seafood. Slice the chicken 1/4 in (3/4 cm) thick and follow recipe exactly.

1. Prepare 7 oz (200 g) pan fried noodles according to instructions. Place on a large platter.

2. Cut prawns in half lengthwise. Slice scallops into ¼ in (¾ cm) thick slices. Combine with salt, wine, egg white and cornstarch. Set aside. Prepare all other ingredients.

3. Heat wok and add 2 T oil and garlic. Stir-fry prawns and scallops until done. (2 min) Remove from wok and set aside.

4. Add 1 T oil to wok, add all vegetables and stir-fry a few seconds. Add soup stock, oyster sauce and salt. Cover, bring to a boil and cook ½ min.

**PRESENTATION**

5. Add seafood to vegetables, thicken with cornstarch mixture and gently stir to combine. Pour ingredients over pan fried noodles or mix noodles with the ingredients in the wok.

## Serve as a wrapper for (as stated in recipe).

### INGREDIENTS: makes 24 pancakes

| | |
|---|---|
| 2 C | all purpose flour |
| ¾ C | boiling water |
| 1-2 T | sesame seed oil |

\* If making wrappers ahead, wrap in foil and freeze. To reheat, allow wrappers to defrost in the foil. Place in a warm oven to reheat. Pancakes may also be steamed to reheat.

★ Mandarin pancakes may be served as a wrapper for:
1. Mu shu pork
2. Chicken with scrambled eggs
3. Shrimp with green peas
4. Beansprouts with pork
Sauce to spread on the wrappers are: Hoisin sauce, plum sauce, hot mustard or any kind of hot sauce.

**PRESENTATION**

1. Place flour in a large bowl, make a well in the center of flour and pour in hot water. Stir with chopsticks until a dough is formed. Knead on a lightly floured surface until smooth. (10 min) Cover dough and let rest for 15 min.

2. On a lightly floured surface, roll out dough ¼ in (¾ cm) thick. Cut 2½ in (6½cm) circles. Continue until all dough is used. Brush half of the circles with oil and stack by two's, like a sandwich. Roll out each pair of circles in a clockwise direction, forming a 6 in (15 cm) circle.

3. Heat a heavy ungreased skillet to 375°F (190°C). Cook pancakes for 1 min, turning over once. (Brown specks are common)

4. While pancakes are still warm, separate halves and stack. Place in a covered dish to keep warm. To serve, fold each pancake into fourths and arrange on a platter.

46

# Meats and Poultry

Meat dishes such as beef, pork and chicken may be combined with vegetables, but will also often be found standing alone as a main course. The meat is usually shredded, sliced, or cubed into succulent bite-sized pieces for convenient serving.

Always bring basic sauce to a full boil, drop in food to be cooked, and then turn the temperature down to simmer. Cover the pot and simmer until done.

## I. *Tofu* (bean curd)

Cut *tofu* (bean curd) into desired size cubes. Bring sauce to a boil, drop in *tofu* (bean curd), turn off heat and allow to steep for 10 min.

**PRESENTATION**

## II. Whole chicken — 3lbs (1500g) — or Cornish Hens

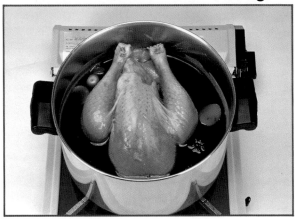 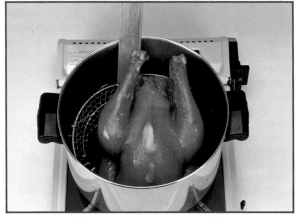

1. Simmer whole chicken in sauce for 20 min. Turn chicken over and simmer 20 min more.

2. Remove from sauce, brush entire chicken with vegetable oil, and allow to cool for 10 min. Cut chicken into bite size pieces and arrange on platter.

## 滷汁 BASIC SAUCE

### INGREDIENTS: makes 5C

| | |
|---|---|
| 2 C | soy sauce |
| ½ C | dark or thick soy sauce |
| 2 C | water |
| ¼ C | rice wine |
| ¼ C | sugar |
| 3 | cloves garlic |
| 3 | whole star anise (1 T) |
| 3 | large slices ginger root |
| 4 | dried chili peppers |
| ¼ C | peanut oil |

* The sauce should be covered and stored in the refrigerator or freezer after each use. After the sauce has been used several times, remove the layer of fat on the surface and replace with ¼ cup fresh oil.
* The flavor of the sauce improves with time and the sauce can be used over and over for months. As the sauce is used, more soy sauce or some of the other ingredients may need to be replenished to keep the proper balance of flavors.

Combine all ingredients of the sauce, bring to a boil, turn down to simmer and cook sauce for 10min. Now sauce is ready to be used to cook whatever meat or vegetable desired.

## Serve with any stir-fried vegetable dish.

## INGREDIENTS: 4 servings

| | |
|---|---|
| 2 | whole chicken breasts or one whole fryer (3 lbs, 1350 g) |
| 2 T | vegetable oil |

**Sauce I**

| | |
|---|---|
| 1/2 C | soup stock |
| 1 T | minced ginger root |
| 2 | cloves garlic, minced |
| 1/2 t | sugar |
| 2 T | soy sauce |
| | |
| 1 t | hot sesame seed oil |

| | |
|---|---|
| 1 | cucumber |
| 1 t | salt |

**Sauce II**

| | |
|---|---|
| 2 T | rice vinegar |
| 1 T | *mirin* |
| 1 T | sugar |

\* Poached Chicken may also be served plain with oyster sauce as a dip.

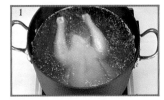

1. Cover chicken with water and bring to a boil. Simmer for 1/2 hour and turn off heat. Allow chicken to poach in the pot until done (15 min). A whole chicken will take a total of 45 min. Remove from pot, brush chicken with 2 T vegetable oil and allow to cool.
2. Combine soup stock, ginger root, garlic, sugar and soy sauce in a pot. Bring to a boil and reduce by half. Allow sauce to cool and add hot sesame seed oil.

3. Cut cucumber and remove seeds. Slice thin and sprinkle with salt. Allow to sit 5 min, rinse and drain. Combine rice vinegar, *mirin* and sugar. Pour over cucumbers. Set aside.
Remove bones from chicken and cut into bite-size pieces. Arrange on a platter and garnish with cucumber slices. Serve Sauce as a dip or pour over chicken pieces.

**PRESENTATION**

## Serve with SPICY BEEF (p. 67).

### INGREDIENTS: 4 servings

| | | | |
|---|---|---|---|
| ³/₄ lb (340 g) | or 1¹/₂ C boneless chicken sliced ¹/₂ in (1¹/₂ cm) thick | 1 T | soy sauce |
| | | 1 t | rice wine |
| 1 | Chinese sausage sliced thin, diagonally | ¹/₂ t | salt |
| 3 | large forest mushrooms | 1 T | cornstarch |
| 25 | dried tiger lily buds | | |

* Vary this recipe with pork, fresh mushrooms, carrots sliced thin, or combine pork with chicken. Also chicken with bone may be used, such as chicken wings or thighs cut in half. Allow longer steaming time for larger pieces of meat. Spareribs are also good. Cut into 1¹/₂ in (4 cm) pieces as for sweet and sour spareribs.

1. Soak mushrooms and tiger lily buds in hot water until soft. Rinse, cut off stems of mushrooms and slice thin. Cut off hard stems of bud and cut buds into 1 in (2¹/₂ cm) pieces.

2. Combine all ingredients well and place in a heatproof plate with a rim.

3. Place in a steamer, bring to a full steam and turn down to medium high. Steam 20 min or until done. Serve in steaming dish.

**PRESENTATION**

## Chow Mein or FRIED RICE (p. 38) would be a good side dish.

### INGREDIENTS: 4-6 servings

| | | | |
|---|---|---|---|
| 2 | chicken breasts | 2 T | rice vinegar |
| 1 t | salt | 3 T | catsup |
| **Batter** | | $^2/_3$ C | sugar |
| $^1/_2$ C | flour | **Garnish** | |
| $^1/_4$ C | cornstarch | 1 | tomato, wedged |
| 1 t | baking powder | 1 | small green pepper, wedged |
| $^1/_2$ t | baking soda | $^1/_2$ C | pineapple chunks |
| $^3/_4$ C | cold water | 1 t | toasted sesame seeds |
| **Sweet and Sour Sauce** | | | |
| $^3/_4$ C | water | 3 C | oil for deep-frying (375°F, |
| 2 T | cornstarch | | 190°C) |

1, Bone chicken and cut into $^1/_2$ in (1$^1/_2$ cm) thick slices.

2. Heat oil in wok to 375°F (190°C). Rub salt into chicken pieces. Dip into batter and deep fry in oil until golden brown. (About 4 min)

3. Bring suace to a full boil stirring constantly. Arrange tomato, pepper and pineapple chunks on top of chicken, pour sauce over and sprinkle sesame seeds on top.

**PRESENTATION**

Serve with PRAWNS WITH VEGETABLES (p. 96).

## INGREDIENTS: 4 servings

| | |
|---|---|
| 1 | fryer chicken (approx. 3 lbs, 1350 g) |
| 1 T | rice wine |
| 1 | clove garlic, minced |
| 1 t | ginger root, minced |
| ½ t | salt |
| ½ t | sugar |
| ½ t | five spice powder |
| 1 T | soy sauce |
| | |
| 3 C | oil for deep-frying (375°F, 190°C) |

* A 14 in (35 cm) wok is best for deep-frying, allowing more depth for the oil and chicken.
* Be sure oil is not too hot: adjust temperature to maintain about 375°F (190°C).
* Chicken can also be baked in the oven at 375°F (140°C) for approximately 1 hour and 10 min.

1. Rinse chicken and dry with paper towels. Place chicken in a large bowl and rub ingredients on chicken in order. Allow to marinate for at least 2 hours.

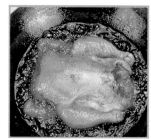

2. Heat about 3 C oil in the wok to 375°F (190°C). Carefully place chicken in wok, breast side down first. Fry chicken for approximately ½ hour, turning often to allow for even browning.

3. Remove from oil and allow to cool 15 min before cutting into bite size pieces.

**PRESENTATION**

# 杏仁鶏 ALMOND BREADED CHICKEN

**Serve with Chow Mein.**

## INGREDIENTS: 4-6 servings

| | | | |
|---|---|---|---|
| 2 | whole chicken breasts | 1 t | *mirin* |
| 1/2 t | salt | 1 T | soy sauce |
| 1 C | panko (dehydrated bread crumb) | | |
| 1/4 C | sliced almonds | 2 C | shredded lettuce |
| 1/2 C | all purpose flour | 1/4 C | toasted, slivered almonds |
| 1 | egg, beaten | | |

3 C  oil for deep-frying (375°F, 190°C)

**Gravy**
1 1/4 C chicken stock
2 T  cornstarch

\* To keep chicken crisp, serve gravy in a separate dish. Almonds can be toasted in the oven at 375°F (190°C) for 10 min. Chicken pieces can be breaded ahead and refrigerated. Chicken thighs or legs can be used instead of breasts.

54

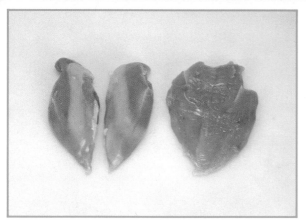

1. Remove bones and skin from chicken breast. Cut each whole chicken breast into halves at the center.

2. **Butterfly** each half by slicing breast from the outer edge, part way through, to open like a book. (The halves will resemble a whole breast, but thinner. This is to enable faster cooking.) Sprinkle ½ t salt over chicken breasts.

3. Combine panko with sliced almonds.

4. Coat each piece of chicken with flour, dip in egg and press on panko mixture.

PRESENTATION

5. Fry in hot oil 375°F (190°C) for 4 min of until golden brown. Cut chicken into bite-size pieces and place on top of a bed of shredded lettuce. Bring gravy to a full boil stirring constantly. Pour over chicken and top with toasted slivered almonds. Serve immediately.

Serve with PEA PODS WITH BEEF (p. 90).

## INGREDIENTS: makes 4-6 servings

| | |
|---|---|
| 2 lbs (900 g) | chicken wings |
| 1 t | salt |
| **Batter** | |
| 1/2 C | all purpose flour |
| 1/4 C | cornstarch |
| 1 t | baking powder |
| 1/2 t | baking soda |
| 3/4 C | cold water |
| | |
| 3 C | oil for deep-frying (375°F, 190°C) |

**Sweet and Sour Dip**
| | |
|---|---|
| 3/4 C | cold water |
| 2 T | cornstarch |
| 2 T | rice vinegar |
| 3 T | catsup |
| 2/3 C | sugar |

**PRESENTATION**

1. Separate wings at joints, discard tips. The larger piece has one bone: remove the meat from the smaller end and push meat up, forming a small drumstick. The flat piece has two bones. Remove the smaller of the two bones. Release the meat from one end and push meat up, forming a small drumstick. Repeat process with other wings.

2. Sprinkle salt over chicken pieces. Combine batter ingredients. Dip each piece into batter (meat only).

3. Heat oil in wok to 375°F (190°C). Deep-fry for 5 min or until done.

4. Bring sauce to a full boil, stirring constantly. Serve as a dip for miniature drumsticks.

## Serve with Steamed Fish and a vegetable dish.

### INGREDIENTS: 4 servings

| | |
|---|---|
| 1¹/₂ lbs (685 g) | chicken thighs cut in half |

**Coat chicken with:**

| | |
|---|---|
| ¹/₂ t | hot pepper |
| 2 t | sesame seed oil |
| 1 T | soy sauce |
| ¹/₂ t | salt |
| ¹/₂ t | sugar |
| 1 t | rice wine |
| 2 t | minced ginger root |
| 1 | clove garlic, minced |

| | |
|---|---|
| 1 | egg yolk |
| ¹/₄ C | cornstarch |
| 3 C | oil for deep-frying (375°F, 190°C) |

**Sauce** (optional)

| | |
|---|---|
| 2 T | soy sauce |
| 1 T | sugar |
| 2 t | sesame seed oil |
| 1 | clove garlic, minced |
| 1 t | minced ginger root |
| ¹/₂ t | hot soy bean paste or chili paste with garlic |
| 1 | green onion, chopped |

**PRESENTATION**

1. Coat chicken pieces and set aside for ¹/₂ hour.

2. Add egg yolk and cornstarch to chicken pieces and mix thoroughly.

3. Deep-fry in hot oil for 5 min. Remove chicken from oil; allow oil to heat back up to 375°F (190°C) and refry chicken for 3 more min.

4. Gently heat sauce until warm and serve if desired.

**Serve with SPICY GROUND PORK (p. 66).**

## INGREDIENTS: 4-6 servings

| | |
|---|---|
| 1 | fryer chicken (approx. 3 lb, 1350 g) |
| 2 T | oil |
| 1 | clove garlic, minced |
| **Sauce** | |
| ¼ C | soy sauce |
| ¼ C | *mirin* |
| ¼ C | water |
| | |
| Some | cornstarch and water for thickening (if needed) |
| 1 | green onion |

\* Chicken parts such as thighs may be substituted.

1. Cut chicken up into pieces about the size of thighs.

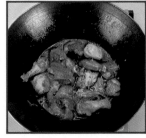

2. Brown chicken in oil on high heat, adding the garlic. (5 min) Drain off excess fat. Add sauce, cover and simmer for 20 min. Turn chicken pieces over once, while simmering.

3. Thicken with cornstarch and water if needed or allow sauce to cook down, forming a glaze. Toss chopped green onions on top of chicken.

**PRESENTATION**

## Delicious with any vegetable dish.

### INGREDIENTS: 4-6 servings

| | |
|---|---|
| 2 lbs (900 g) | chicken wings or thighs |
| 1 T | soy sauce |
| 1 | clove garlic, minced |
| 1 t | minced ginger root |
| 2 T | oil |
| | |
| 3 T | oyster sauce |
| 1 T | *mirin* |
| 1/2 t | salt |
| 1 C | water |
| 2 t | sesame seed oil |
| Some | cornstarch and water for thickening |
| | |
| 1 | bunch spinach, blanched |

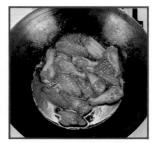

1. Cut chicken wings into individual parts, discarding tips. If using thighs, cut in half.

2. Combine chicken pieces with soy sauce, garlic and ginger. Set aside for 1/2 hour. Heat wok and add 2 T oil. Lightly brown chicken on high heat, drain excess oil from wok.

3. Add oyster sauce, *mirin*, salt and water. Cover, bring to boil and turn temperature down. Cook 15 to 20 min. Turn temperature to high, add sesame seed oil, thicken with cornstarch to make a medium thick gravy.

4. Arrange the blanched spinach on a platter and serve chicken pieces on top.

**POACHED WHOLE FISH (p. 78)** would be a good accompaniment.

## INGREDIENTS: 4 servings

| | |
|---|---|
| 1½ lbs (685 g) | chicken parts (wings or thighs) |
| 2 T | oil |
| 1 | clove garlic, crushed |
| 2 T | hoisin sauce |
| ½ t | salt |
| ½ C | water or soup stock |
| 1 | green onion, chopped |

\* Boneless chicken may be used. Reduce browning time. Spareribs are also good. Use 1½ in (4 cm) pieces as for SWEET AND SOUR SPARERIBS (pg. 62).

**PRESENTATION**

Separate wings at joints, discard tips. If using thighs, chop in half. Heat oil in wok and brown meat on all sides, turning temperature down if too hot (10 min). Add crushed garlic and fry ½ min. Drain off excess fat. Add hoisin sauce, salt and water. Cover, bring to a boil and cook until most of liquid has evaporated (about 5 min). Reduce temperature if liquid is cooking off too fast. Garnish with green onions and serve hot.

Serve with stir-fried vegetables or any noodle dish.

## INGREDIENTS: 4 servings

| | |
|---|---|
| 1 | side of pork spareribs (lean) 3lbs (1350g) |
| 1 t | salt |
| 1 T | Chinese wine |

**Marinade**

| | |
|---|---|
| 1/4 C | hoisin sauce |
| 1/4 C | catsup |
| 1 T | *mirin* |
| 2 T | sugar |
| 1 t | minced ginger root |
| 1 | clove garlic, minced |

**PRESENTATION**

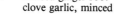

1. Mix together marinade. Rub salt and wine on ribs.

2. Spread marinade on both sides of the spareribs. Marinate about 2 hours.

3. Place ribs on rack of broiler pan with water in bottom of pan.

4. Roast for 1 hour and 15 min or until done at 375°F (190°C). Turn and baste as needed. Cut into bite size pieces or leave as whole ribs.

61

## Delicious with ALMOND BREADED CHICKEN (p. 54).

## INGREDIENTS: 4 servings

| | |
|---|---|
| 2 lbs (900 g) | spareribs |
| 1 T | oil |
| **Sauce** | |
| 3/4 C | water |
| 2 T | cornstarch |
| 2 T | soy sauce |
| 3 T | rice vinegar |
| 2/3 | sugar |
| **Garnish** | |

tomato, green pepper, pineapple chunks and toasted sesame seeds

\* Pork cubes may be used in this recipe. This dish keeps warm very well. For sweet and sour fried pork: follow recipe for sweet and sour chicken.

**PRESENTATION**

1. Cut spareribs into 1½ in (4 cm) pieces.

2. Brown ribs in oil for 5 min and drain excess oil.

3. Mix sauce ingredients together.

4. Add to spareribs, stirring constantly until sauce thickens. Cover and simmer for ½ hour. Garnish with tomato, green pepper, pineapple chunks and toasted sesame seeds.

## STIR-FRIED GEODUCK WITH VEGETABLES (p. 80) would be a good complement.

### INGREDIENTS: 4 servings

| | | | |
|---|---|---|---|
| 1¹/₂ lbs (685 g) | spareribs cut into 1¹/₂ in (4 cm) pieces | 2 t | dark soy sauce |
| 1 T | o i l | 1 T | *mirin* |
| 1 T | salted black beans, rinsed | ¹/₄ t | salt |
| 2 | cloves garlic | ¹/₂ t | sugar |
| 1 t | ginger root | 1 t | cornstarch dissolved in 1 t water |
| 1 C | soup stock | Some | chopped green onions |

\* Pork cubes may be used instead of spareribs.

**PRESENTATION**

1. Brown spareribs in oil on high heat for 5 min. Drain excess fat.

2. Mash black beans, garlic and ginger. Add to spareribs and cook ¹/₂ min.

3. Add soup stock, soy sauce, *mirin*, salt and sugar. Cover and simmer 15 to 20 min.

4. There should be small amount of liquid left. Add cornstarch mixture to thicken. Garnish with green onions.

# 叉燒 BARBECUED PORK

Good with any rice or noodle dish.

## INGREDIENTS: 4 servings

2½-3 lbs (1125-1350 g) boneless pork (pork loin or tenderloin)
**Marinade**
| | |
|---|---|
| 1½ t | salt |
| 1 T | rice wine |
| ½ t | garlic powder |
| 2 T | hoisin sauce |
| ¼ C | catsup |
| ¼ C | sugar |
| 3 | drops red food coloring (optional) |

Some paper clips to hang pork strips

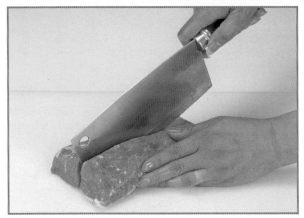

1. Cut pork into strips 2½ × 2 × 7 in (6½ × 5 × 18 cm). Some pieces may vary in length.

2. Marinate pork strips at least 2 hours or overnight in the refrigerator.

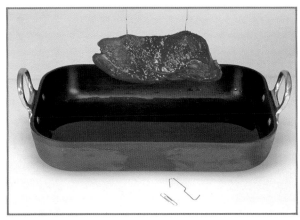

3. Separate both racks of oven as far apart as possible to hang the pork strips. Unwind paper clips to form hooks. Hook each strip of pork in the center, and hang from the top rack of the oven over a pan of water in the lower rack. Roast at 350°F (175°C) for 1 hour or until done.

4. Allow to cool. Slice into ¼ in (¾ cm) slices. Serve with hot mustard, toasted sesame seeds and hot catsup.

Pork strips may also be roasted on a rack over a pan of water without hanging. Be sure to turn pork at least once.

* Hot mustard is purchased as a powder. To prepare, combine 1 T mustard to 1 T water and stir until smooth. Hot catsup: Combine prepared hot mustard with catsup to desired hotness.
* Any cut of pork may be used, but tenderness will vary according to cut. Best to use boneless pork loin or tenderloin. Tougher cuts require longer cooking time. Pork strips keep well frozen in whole piece after roasting. Reheat if desired and slice before serving.

**PRESENTATION**

Serve with POACHED WHOLE FISH (p. 78)

## INGREDIENTS: 4 servings

| | |
|---|---|
| 1 T | oil |
| 1 clove | garlic, minced |
| 1 t | minced ginger root |
| 1/2 lb (225 g) | lean ground pork |
| 1 | Chinese sausage chopped |
| 1 | small onion chopped |
| 1/4 C | forest mushrooms chopped |
| 3 T | hoisin sauce |
| 2 T | catsup |
| 1 T | sugar |
| 1 T | chili paste with soy bean |
| 1 t | soy sauce |
| | salt to taste |

| | |
|---|---|
| 1/4 C | water |
| Some | cornstarch for thickening |
| 1 | green onion, chopped |
| 1 | lettuce for cups |

1. Heat oil in wok and cook pork and sausage, drain off excess fat.

2. Add onions and mushrooms, cook for 1 min.

3. Add remaining ingredients and thicken with cornstarch mixture. Add green onions. Serve minced pork mixture wrapped with lettuce.

**PRESENTATION**

## Start the meal with a light soup.

### INGREDIENTS: 4 servings

| | | | |
|---|---|---|---|
| ¹/₂ lb (225 g) | beef steak | 1 | green pepper cut into shreds |
| 2 t | soy sauce | 1 t | rice wine |
| 1 t | sugar | ¹/₂ t | sugar |
| 2 t | cornstarch | ¹/₂ t | salt |
| 2 T | oil | 1 t | sesame seed oil |
| | | 1¹/₂ T | hoisin sauce (optional) |
| 1 T | oil | ¹/₄ C | shredded green onions |
| 1 clove | garlic, minced | | |
| 1 t | minced ginger root | | |
| 1¹/₂ t | hot bean paste | | |

\* Serve this dish with lettuce cups, use the small inside leaves of a head of lettuce as a cup. Scoop some beef into the cup and eat like a sandwich.
\* Substitute shredded carrots for the green pepper.

1. Slice beef thin against the grain. Then cut into shreds to resemble bean sprouts. Coat beef with soy sauce, sugar and cornstarch.

2. Heat wok, add 2 T oil and stir-fry beef until done. Remove from wok and set aside.

3. Add 1 T oil to wok, fry garlic, ginger and hot bean paste for a few seconds. Add shredded green pepper and stir to combine ingredients. Add rice wine, sugar, salt and sesame seed oil. Stir in hoisin sauce if desired. Return beef to wok, mix in green onions and cook ¹/₂ min to thoroughly combine ingredients.

**PRESENTATION**

67

## Serve with plain vegetable dish accompanied with white rice.

### INGREDIENTS: 4 servings

$1^1/_2$-2lbs (685-900 g) tender steak

**Sauce**

| | |
|---|---|
| $^1/_3$ C | soy sauce |
| $^1/_4$ C | *mirin* |
| 2 cloves | garlic |
| $^1/_6$ oz (5 g) | ginger |

1. Chop ginger and mince garlic.

2. Marinate steaks for one hour in the sauce.

3. Broil steaks until done. Slice in to $^1/_2$ in ($1^1/_2$ cm) thick slices to serve. Bring remaining sauce to a boil, pour sauce over slices of steak.

**PRESENTATION**

68

White rice with a simple vegetable dish such as CHINESE GREENS WITH CHICKEN (p. 92).

## INGREDIENTS: 4 servings

| | |
|---|---|
| 1 lb (450 g) | flank steak sliced thin against the grain |
| 2 t | soy sauce |
| 2 t | cornstarch |
| 1 t | sugar |
| 2 t | rice wine |
| | |
| 2 T | oil |
| 8 | slices ginger root |
| | |
| $\frac{1}{2}$ C | soup stock |
| $\frac{1}{2}$ t | sugar |
| $\frac{1}{2}$ t | salt or to taste |
| Some | cornstarch and water for thickening |

\* Other cuts of beef may be used instead of flank steak.

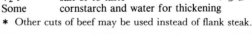

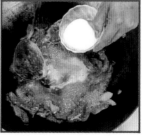

**PRESENTATION**

1. Mix meat with soy sauce, cornstarch, sugar and wine. Set aside.

2. Heat wok and add the oil. Add ginger slices, fry about $\frac{1}{2}$ min on high heat. Add beef, cook about 1 min or until done. Push meat up the side of the wok.

3. Add soup stock, sugar and salt. Bring to a boil, thicken with cornstarch mixture.

Serve with DEEP-FRIED PRAWNS (p. 82).

## INGREDIENTS: 4 servings

| | |
|---|---|
| 1 lb (450g) | flank steak |
| 1 T | cornstarch |
| 1 T | soy sauce |
| 1 t | sugar |
| 1/2 lb (225g) | fresh mushrooms |
| 1 T | oil |
| | |
| 2 T | oil |
| 2 T | oyster sauce |
| 1/2 C | water |
| 1 T | cornstarch dissolved in 1 T water |

\* Blanch one bunch of tender spinach, place on platter and serve with beef poured over spinach.

**PRESENTATION**

1. Slice steak 1/4 in (3/4 cm) thick against the grain. Mix with cornstarch, soy sauce and sugar. Set aside. Slice mushrooms 1/4 in (3/4 cm) thick.

2. Heat wok and add 1 T oil. Stir-fry the mushrooms for 1 min on high heat, remove and set aside.

3. Heat wok with the remaining 2 T oil and stir-fry the beef until done. Add oyster sauce and water, bring to a boil. Add salt to taste if desired. Thicken with cornstarch and water. Add mushrooms, stir to combine ingredients.

# Seafoods

Nowhere is the importance of bringing out the natural flavor of food more evident than in the preparation of fish and shellfish. The key to delicious seafood is freshness. Fresh fish will exhibit firm flesh, round clear eyes, bright red gills, and a mild fresh odor.

## Serve with CHICKEN WITH ALMONDS (p. 89).

### INGREDIENTS: 4 servings

| | |
|---|---|
| 1¹/₂ lbs (685 g) | fish steaks or fillets |
| ¹/₄ C | red *miso* (soy bean paste) |
| 1 T | slivered ginger root |
| 1 T | sesame seed oil |
| 2 | green onions, chopped |
| 2 T | oil (heated until hot) |

\* This recipe is good to use with any kind of fish steaks or fillets. Omit the hot oil to reduce calories.

1. Clean fish and dry with paper towel. Place in a heatproof plate with a rim. Spread a thin layer of *miso* over the top of the pieces of fish. Sprinkle with ginger and sesame seed oil.

2. Place on a steamer and steam for 15 to 20 min.

3. Toss green onions over fish and sizzle with hot oil.

**PRESENTATION**

EGG FU YUNG (p. 100) would be a nice complement.

## INGREDIENTS: 4 servings

| | |
|---|---|
| 1¹/₂ lbs (685 g) | white fish fillets |
| ¹/₈ t | white pepper |
| 2 T | sesame seed oil |
| ¹/₄ C | soy sauce |
| 1 T | slivered fresh ginger root |
| ¹/₄ C | slivered green onions |
| ¹/₄ C | oil (heated until hot) |

\* If fish is thin, shape into rolls.

**PRESENTATION**

1. Clean and thoroughly dry fish with paper towel. Place fish in a heatproof plate and place in a steamer. Steam fish about 10 min for 1 in (2¹/₂ cm) of thickness.

2. Remove fish from steamer, pour out excess liquid.

3. Sprinkle with pepper, sesame seed oil, soy sauce, ginger root and green onion. Pour hot oil over fish to sizzle ingredients.

# 甜酸魚 SWEET AND SOUR FISH

Serve with stir-fried vegetable.

## INGREDIENTS: 4-6 servings

| | | | |
|---|---|---|---|
| 1 | fish (2-3 lb, 900-1350 g rock cod, sea bass or fillets) | 2 T | oil |
| | | 1 | clove garlic, minced |
| 1 T | wine | 1 T | slivered ginger root |
| 1 t | salt | 4 | medium forest mushrooms (soaked, rinsed and sliced) |
| ½ C | all purpose flour | 1 | carrot, peeled and slivered |
| ½ C | cornstarch | | |
| 2 | eggs, beaten | ½ C | slivered green peppers |
| | | 2 | green onions, slivered |

**Sauce**

| | |
|---|---|
| 5 C | oil for deep-frying |
| ¼ C | rice vinegar |
| ¼ C | sugar |
| 3 T | catsup |
| ½ t | chili pepper |
| 1 T | rice wine |
| ¼ t | salt |
| 1 t | sesame seed oil |
| ½ C | water |
| 5 t | cornstarch |

1. Clean and dry fish. Cut 3 slashes on both sides of the fish, 1 in (2½ cm) apart. Rub with wine and salt.

2. Combine flour and cornstarch. Coat fish with mixture. Dip in eggs, then again in flour mixture.

3. Fry in 375°F (190°C) oil for 15 min turning once. Remove and place on a platter.

4. Heat 2 T oil in wok, fry garlic, ginger, mushrooms, carrots, and green peppers for ½ min.

5. Add all sauce ingredients, stir and bring to a boil, adding green onions. Serve sauce over fish.

**PRESENTATION**

Serve with steamed hot white rice.

## INGREDIENTS: 4 servings

| | |
|---|---|
| 1 | large cooked crab (2$^1/_2$lbs, 1125g) |
| | |
| 1$^1/_2$T | fermented black beans, rinsed and drained |
| 2 | cloves garlic, crushed |
| 2 | slices ginger root |
| 1t | sugar |
| 1T | oil |
| $^1/_2$lb (225g) | ground pork |
| | |
| 2T | oyster sauce |
| $^1/_4$t | salt |
| 1C | water |
| 1 | egg |
| 2 | green onions, chopped |
| Some | cornstarch and water for thickening |

\* Uncooked lobster tails may be substituted for the crab. Devein tails and cut into individual sections, shells intact. Follow recipe and add lobster after cooking the pork. Do **not** remove lobster from the wok during cooking.

76

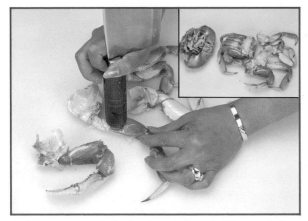

1. Remove outer shell of crab and discard. Rinse and clean crab. Cut crab in half. Holding each leg by the cavity, break off a section of the center cavity with each leg. Crack legs, rinse off bits of shell, drain and set aside.

2. Mash black beans with garlic, ginger and sugar. Set aside.

3. Heat wok and add oil. Stir-fry pork on high heat until done (about 2 min). If there is excess fat from the pork, drain off.

4. Add black bean mixture and mix together with pork. Add oyster sauce, salt and water. Stir to combine. Carefully place crab on top, cover wok, bring to a boil and cook 3 to 4 min to heat crab through.

**PRESENTATION**

5. Carefully remove crab pieces and place on a platter. Add egg to mixture in the wok and stir. Toss in green onions and thicken with cornstarch and water mixture. Pour entire mixture (called lobster sauce) over the crab.

## Serve with stir-fried broccoli.

### INGREDIENTS: 4-6 servings

| | |
|---|---|
| 1 | sea bass, cleaned (retain head and tail) |
| 1 | green onion |
| 2 | slices ginger root |
| | |
| ¼ t | white pepper |
| ¼ C | soy sauce |
| 1 T | sesame seed oil |
| ¼ C | slivered, pickled ginger and vegetables |
| 2 | green onions, slivered in 2 in (5 cm) lengths |
| ¼ C | oil (heated until hot) |

* Use about 2 T of fresh slivered ginger root instead of pickled ginger and vegetables, if desired.
* Pickled ginger and vegetables are sold in cans. Once opened, keep in a jar sealed tightly in the refrigerator. Keeps for several weeks.
* Any firm fish can be cooked this way. Try this recipe with salmon steaks or fillets. Be sure to adjust poaching time so fish does not over-cook.

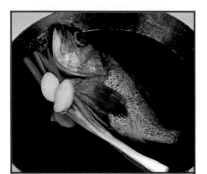

### PRESENTATION

1. In a large pot, bring to a boil enough water to cover the fish. Add ginger, green onion and the fish. Cover pot, turn temperature to the lowest setting and poach 25 min or until done. Remove fish carefully with a large metal strainer and spatula. Place on a large platter.

2. Sprinkle white pepper over fish. Pour soy sauce and sesame seed oil on top of fish. Arrange pickles and green onions on top of fish. Heat the ¼ C oil until hot and pour over fish and green onions. The ingredients should sizzle.

Serve with *Tofu* soup (p. 28).

## INGREDIENTS: 4 servings

| | | | |
|---|---|---|---|
| 1½ lbs (685 g) | clams in shells (24 clams) | 1 T | *mirin* |
| 1½ T | black beans | 1 T | rice wine |
| 1 | large clove garlic | 1 t | chili paste with soy bean |
| 2 | thin slices of ginger root | ½ t | salt |
| | | ½ C | water |
| 2 T | oil | 1 | green onion, chopped |
| 2 t | soy sauce | Some | cornstarch for thickening |

✳ Clams can also be soaked overnight in cold water with some corn meal to remove sand. Use scallops or fish as a substitute for clams. If scallops are small, leave whole. Slice fish into $1 \times 2 \times \frac{1}{2}$ in ($2\frac{1}{2} \times 5 \times 1\frac{1}{2}$ cm) slices.

### PREPARE

Soak clams in cold water with an iron knife for 4 hours to remove sand. Remove clams, rinse and drain. Rinse black beans, drain. Mash beans with garlic and ginger to form a paste.

1. Heat oil in wok until hot, add clams and stir fry a few seconds. Add black bean mixture to the bottom of wok and stir-fry ½ min.

2. Add soy sauce, *mirin* rice wine, chili paste, salt and water. Cover, bring to a full boil and steam 3 min. Add green onions and thicken with cornstarch and water to desired consistency.

### PRESENTATION

HOISIN SAUCE CHICKEN (p. 60) is a good side dish.

## INGREDIENTS: 4-6 servings

| | | | |
|---|---|---|---|
| 1 | medium geoduck clam | $^1/_2$ lb (225 g) | pea pods |
| 1 T | rice wine | | (stringed, rinsed and |
| $^1/_2$ t | salt | | drained) |
| $^1/_4$ t | white pepper | 1 | small onion cut in |
| 1 t | sesame seed oil | | wedges |
| 2 t | cornstarch | $^1/_4$ C | sliced water chestnuts |
| | | $^1/_4$ C | sliced bamboo shoots |
| 3 T | oil | $^1/_2$ t | salt |
| 2 cloves garlic, minced | | 2 T | soup stock or water |
| | | 1 T | slivered ginger root |
| | | 2 t | soy sauce |
| | | 1 T | rice wine |
| | | 2 | green onions cut into |
| | | | 1 in (2$^1/_2$ cm) pieces |

**✳** Substitute clam slices with $^1/_2$ lb (225 g) scallops sliced $^1/_4$ in ($^3/_4$ cm) thick.

1. Place geoduck in the sink and run hot water on the neck of the clam until the skin separates from the neck. Run a knife around the inside of the shell to open the clam.

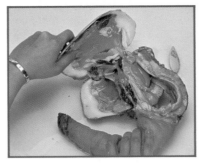

2. Discard stomach and pull off neck.

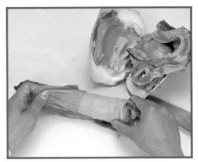

3. Rinse carefully to remove sand and skin.

4. Cut off the very tip of the neck and slice open lengthwise.

5. Make incisions lengthwise.

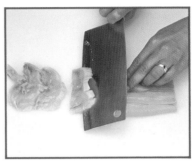

6. Slice into thin ⅛ in (½ cm) slices.

7. Combine with rice wine, salt, pepper, sesame seed oil and cornstarch.

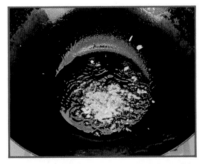

8. Heat wok and add 1 T oil. Add some of the garlic and allow to fry for a few seconds.

9. Add vegetables and salt. Stir-fry for about 1 min, adding soup stock if necessary. Remove to a platter.

10. Clean wok. Heat wok and add 2 T oil. Fry garlic and ginger for a few seconds. Add clam slices and stir-fry for about ½ min. Add soy sauce and wine.

11. Toss in green onions. Salt to taste and serve over vegetables. Do not overcook clam slices or they will be tough.

**PRESENTATION**

Delicious with SWEET AND SOUR SAUCE (p. 11).

## INGREDIENTS: 4 servings

| | |
|---|---|
| 1 lb (450 g) | prawns (24 prawns) |
| ½ t | salt |
| **Batter** | |
| ½ C | all purpose flour |
| ¼ C | cornstarch |
| 1 t | baking powder |
| ½ t | baking soda |
| ⅔ C | cold water |
| | |
| 3 C | oil for deep-frying (375°F, 190°C) |
| | |
| 1 | lemon cut into wedges |
| Some | Chinese hot mustard and catsup |

* Hot mustard is purchased as a powder. To prepare, combine 1 T mustard to 1 T water and stir until smooth.
* Hot catsup: Combine prepared hot mustard with catsup to desired hotness. The above batter is excellent for fish or other shellfish. Cut fish into 3 in (8 cm) pieces. Be sure to towel dry fish or other shellfish or batter will not adhere.
* **Sweet & Sour Prawns:** Serve with sweet and sour sauce garnished with tomato, green pepper and pineapple chunks.

Shell prawns, retaining the tail. Open top of prawn just enough to remove the vein. Rinse and dry prawns with paper towels. Salt prawns. Mix together the batter. Heat 3 C of oil in the wok to 375°F (190°C). Dip prawns into batter and deep-fry prawns for 2 to 3 min or until golden brown. Serve with lemon wedges, hot mustard and hot catsup.

**PRESENTATION**

Serve with BON BON CHICKEN (p. 50).

## INGREDIENTS: 4 servings

| | |
|---|---|
| ¾ lb (340 g) | prawns |
| 2 T | oil |
| 1 clove | garlic, minced |
| 1 t | minced ginger root |
| 2 t | hot bean paste |
| ¼ C | catsup |
| 3 T | rice wine |
| ½ t | salt |
| 1 T | sugar |
| ¼ C | chopped onions |

✳ The shell of the prawn is in sections. If the vein breaks, go to the next section and try to remove the vein. If this is too difficult, cook the prawns shelled. The shell of the prawn retains the moisture when cooked.

**PRESENTATION**

1. Remove vein from the top of the prawns carefully. Rinse and pat dry (do not shell the prawns).

2. Heat wok and oil. Add prawns, garlic and ginger. Stir-fry 1 min.

3. Add hot bean paste, catsup, wine, salt and sugar. Bring to a boil, cooking prawns (1 min). Toss in green onions.

# 蝦龍糊 PRAWNS WITH LOBSTER SAUCE

Serve with Chinese Greens with Beef. (Variation of CHINESE GREENS WITH CHICKEN, p. 92)

## INGREDIENTS: 4 servings

| | |
|---|---|
| 1 lb (450 g) | prawns |
| 1½ T | fermented black beans, rinsed and drained |
| 1 clove | garlic, crushed |
| 1 | slice ginger root |
| 1 t | sugar |
| 3 T | oil |
| ½ lb (225 g) | ground pork |
| 2 t | hot bean paste |
| 2 T | oyster sauce |
| ¼ t | salt |
| ⅔ C | water |
| 1 | egg |
| 1 | green onion, chopped |
| Some | cornstarch and water for thickening |

\* The above recipe has no lobster but is called lobster sauce because traditionally lobster was cooked in combination with the pork and black beans.

1. Shell prawns retaining tails. Devein and rinse. Slice prawns in half lengthwise, at the top end only (butterfly).

2. Mash black beans with garlic, ginger and sugar. Set aside.

3. Add 3 T oil to wok and stir-fry the pork about 2 min or until the pink color is gone.

4. Add black bean mixture, stir to combine.

5. Add prawns and cook ½ min.

6. If you like, add hot bean paste.

7. Add oyster sauce, salt and water. Bring to a boil, cover wok and cook 1 min.

8. Stir in egg, and add green onions and thicken with cornstarch and water mixture.

**PRESENTATION**

## Serve with BROILED GINGER STEAK (p. 68).

### INGREDIENTS: 4 servings

| | |
|---|---|
| 2 oz (60 g) | bean threads, soaked |
| 1 | cucumber, shredded |
| 2 C | shredded lettuce |
| 1 C | cooked tiny shrimp |
| or | |
| 1 | cooked chicken breast shredded |
| 1/4 C | chopped green onions |

**Dressing**

| | | | |
|---|---|---|---|
| 2 T | sesame seed paste or chunky peanut butter | | |
| 2 t | fresh minced ginger root | | |
| 1 T | chopped green onions | 1 t | sugar |
| 2 cloves | garlic, minced | 1 t | sesame seed oil |
| 1 T | soy sauce | 1 t | hot pepper oil |
| 1/4 C | soup stock | 1 t | rice vinegar |

**PRESENTATION**

1. Bring a pot of water to a boil and cook bean threads for 2 min.

2. Rinse bean threads in cold water and drain thoroughly. Place in a large platter.

3. Arrange all other ingredients on top.

4. Combine ingredients of dressing. Pour it on just before serving.

86

# Vegetables, Eggs and Tofu

These ingredients are essential to a variety of meatless and almost meatless courses. In addition, they are very economical to buy and high in nutritional content. A multitude of vegetables are available through your local markets.

Fresh *tofu* (bean curd) is sold in 12-16 oz (340-450 g) creamy white blocks. *Tofu* is rich in protein, vitamins and minerals, but low in calories, saturated fats, and free of cholesterol.

**Serve EGG ROLLS (p. 12) as a side dish.**

## INGREDIENTS: 4-6 servings

| | |
|---|---|
| 3 C | oil for deep-frying |
| 2½ oz (70 g) | maifun (rice sticks) |
| 3 | forest mushrooms |
| 1 C | cooked, shredded chicken breast |
| 2 C | shredded lettuce |
| ¼ C | chopped green onions |
| 1 T | toasted sesame seeds |
| ½ C | toasted slivered almonds |
| **Dressing** | |
| ¼ C | rice vinegar |
| ¼ C | vegetable oil |
| 1 t | sesame seed oil |
| 2 T | sugar |
| ¼ t | black pepper |
| ½ t | salt |

1. Heat 3 C oil in the wok to 400°F (205°C). Put in one rice stick. If it puffs up immediately, put in a small handful. Turn rice sticks over to allow the sticks on top to puff. Remove immediately. Set aside.

2. Soak mushrooms until soft, rinse and boil in some water for 10 min. Remove and allow to cool. Squeeze dry and slice into thin strips. Have all other ingredients cut and ready. Combine all ingredients and toss with dressing just before serving.

**TIP**

**A ·** An easy way to cook the chicken breast is to poach in water until done, about half an hour. Bring water to a boil first, add chicken breast, cover pot and simmer for ½ hour.

**B ·** To toast almonds: Place in 350°F (175°C) oven and bake 10 min.

## Serve with any meat dish.

### INGREDIENTS: 4 servings

| | |
|---|---|
| 1 | chicken breast, boned and diced |
| 6 | large prawns (shelled, deveined, rinsed and diced) |
| 1 | small onion, diced |
| 1 | celery stalk, diced |
| 1/2 C | diced bamboo shoots |
| 1/4 C | diced water chestnuts |
| 1/2 C | button mushrooms |
| 2 T | oil |
| 1/2 C | frozen green peas, defrosted |
| 1 T | *mirin* |
| 1 t | salt |
| 1/2 C | soup stock |
| Some | cornstarch and water for thickening |
| 1/2 C | toasted whole almonds |

∗ Pork may be substituted for the chicken. Use other vegetables such as diced green beans, asparagus, broccoli stems, carrots or peppers.
∗ Cashew nuts may be used instead of almonds. Toast almonds in the oven for 10-15 min at 350°F (175°C).

1. All meats and vegetables should be diced in 1/2 in (1¹/₂ cm) cubes.

2. Heat wok, add 2 T oil and stir-fry the chicken for 2 min on high heat. Add prawns and stir-fry for 1/2 min.

3. Add all ingredients except cornstarch and almonds. Cover wok, bring to a boil and cook 1 min. Thicken with cornstarch mixture. Remove to a serving dish and garnish with toasted almonds on top.

### PRESENTATION

# 雪豆牛肉 PEA PODS WITH BEEF Vegetables, Eggs and *Tofu*

## Serve with STUFFED MUSHROOMS (p. 94).

### INGREDIENTS: 4 servings

| | |
|---|---|
| 1 lb (450g) | fresh pea pods |
| 1/4 lb (115g) | beef |
| 1 t | soy sauce |
| 1/2 t | sugar |
| 1 t | cornstarch |
| 3 T | oil |
| 1 clove | garlic, minced |
| 1 T | oyster sauce |
| 1/4 t | salt or to taste |
| 1/4 C | soup stock |
| Some | cornstarch and water for thickening if needed |

\* Most any vegetable can be used in the above recipe. Prepare vegetable for cooking and adjust cooking time and soup stock needed according to how long the vegetable needs to be cooked to be crisp tender.

\* Substitute other meats for beef to obtain a variation of this dish.

1. Slice beef thinly against the grain. Break tips of pea pods and remove strings. Rinse and drain. Combine beef with soy sauce, sugar and corn-starch. Set aside.

2. Heat wok, add 1 1/2 T oil, garlic and the beef. Stir-fry the beef until done, remove and set aside.

3. Add 1 1/2 T oil to wok. Stir-fry pea pods for 1/2 min. Add oyster sauce, salt and soup stock. Bring to a boil, cooking pea pods just until tender (1/2 min). Add beef to pea pods. Thicken with corn-starch and water mixture to form a medium thick sauce if desired.

### PRESENTATION

90

## Delicious as a complete meal served with hot steamed white rice.

### INGREDIENTS: 4 servings

| | |
|---|---|
| ½ lb (225 g) | flank steak, sliced thin against the grain |
| 2 t | cornstarch |
| 2 t | soy sauce |
| ½ t | sugar |
| 1½ lbs (685 g) | broccoli |
| 2 T | oil |
| ½ t | salt |
| ½ C | soup stock |
| Some | cornstarch for thickening |

\* This recipe is good for dense vegetable such as cauliflower, green beans and asparagus.

**Cauliflower:** Separate into flowerets. Slice into ½ in (1½ cm) thick slices.

**Green Beans:** String the beans and cut into 2 in (5 cm) lengths. If the beans are too thick, cut into ½ in (1½ cm) thick diagonal slices.

**Asparagus:** Snap off ends of asparagus and slice into ½ in (1½ cm) thick diagonal slices.

1. Combine beef with cornstarch, soy sauce and sugar. Set aside. Cut broccoli flowerets into 2 in (5 cm) lengths, separating into small clusters. Peel stem and cut in ½ in (1½ cm) thick diagonal slices.

2. Heat wok, add oil and stir-fry beef slices on high heat until doen. Remove and set aside.

3. Add broccoli to wok. Add salt and soup stock. Cover wok, bring to a boil and cook 2-3 min. Then return beef to wok and thicken with cornstarch mixture. Stir to combine all ingredients.

**PRESENTATION**

A fish dish would make a good accompaniment.

## INGREDIENTS: 2 servings

| | |
|---|---|
| $1/2$ lb (225 g) | chicken |
| 2 t | cornstarch |
| 2 t | soy sauce |
| 1 t | sugar |
| $1^1/_2$ lbs (685 g) | Chinese greens (bok choy) |
| 3 T | oil |
| $1/_2$ C | soup stock |
| $1/_2$ t | salt |
| 2 t | cornstarch dissolved in 1 T water |

* Other vegetables may be substituted. Adjust steaming time and soup stock.
* Dense vegetables such as broccoli require longer cooking, more soup stock required.

1. Slice chicken ¼ in (¾ cm) thick against the grain. Marinate chicken in cornstarch, soy sauce and sugar.

2. Cut bok choy in ½ in (1½ cm) diagonal slices.

3. Heat 2 T oil in wok and stir-fry chicken on high heat until done; remove from wok and set aside.

4. Add 1 T oil and stir-fry bok choy on high heat for ½ min. Add soup stock, salt, cover bring to boil and steam 1 min.

5. Return chicken to wok and mix, add enough cornstarch mixture to thicken. Serve with white rice.

**PRESENTATION**

# 釀鮮菇 STUFFED MUSHROOMS

Serve with SWEET AND SOUR CHICKEN (p. 52).

## INGREDIENTS: 4-6 servings

| | | | |
|---|---|---|---|
| 1½ lbs (685 g) | fresh mushrooms (24 medium) | 1 T | oil |
| **Filling** | | 1 T | *mirin* or sherry |
| ½ lb (225 g) | lean ground pork | 1 T | oyster sauce |
| ¼ lb (115 g) | fresh prawns (shelled, deveined, rinsed and chopped | 2 t | soy sauce |
| | | ½ C | soup stock |
| 4 | water chestnuts, chopped | Some | cornstarch and water for thickening |
| 2 T | chopped bamboo shoots | 1 | green onion, chopped |
| 1 t | minced ginger root (optional) | | |
| 1 t | soy sauce | | |
| 1 t | rice wine | | |
| ½ t | salt | | |
| ¼ t | white pepper | | |
| 1 T | cornstarch | | |

\* Use smaller mushrooms and serve as an appetizer.

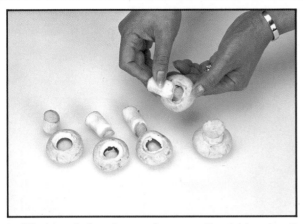

1. Wash and dry the mushrooms. Gently break off stems and reserve for another use.

2. Combine all filling ingredients.

3. Stuff mushrooms, dividing filling equally. Use about 1½ t for each mushrooms.

4. Mushrooms are stuffed.

5. Heat a slillet and add oil. Lightly brown mushrooms, meat side down over medium heat. Turn mushrooms over and cook tops for about 1 min. Add *mirin*, oyster sauce, soy sauce and soup stock. Cover, bring to a boil and simmer for about 10 min. Thicken with cornstarch and water mixture. Add green onions.

**PRESENTATION**

95

# PRAWNS WITH VEGETABLES

Very good with Chinese Style Fried Chicken.

## INGREDIENTS: 4 servings

| | |
|---|---|
| 1 | small carrot |
| ¹/₂ lb (225 g) | prawns |
| 1 | small onion, wedged |
| 2 | large forest mushrooms (soaked, rinsed and sliced) |
| 1 C | sliced fresh mushrooms |
| 1 | small green pepper |
| ¹/₄ C | sliced bamboo shoots |
| ¹/₄ C | sliced water chestnuts |
| 3 T | oil |
| ¹/₂ t | salt or to taste |
| 1 T | rice wine |
| ¹/₂ C | soup stock |
| 2 t | cornstarch dissolved in 2 T water |

1. Chop carrot with mold.

2. Slice thin diagonally.

3. Shell prawns, devein, and rinse.

4. Cut prawns in half lengthwise.

5. All ingredients are prepared.

6. Heat wok, add 2 T oil. Stir-fry prawns for 2 min or until done. Remove and set aside.

7. Add 1 T oil to the wok and stir-fry all vegetables, adding the salt, rice wine and soup stock. Cover, bring to a boil and cook 1/2 min.

8. Add prawns to the vegetables, thicken with cornstarch mixture and stir to combine all ingredients.

**PRESENTATION**

# 木須肉 **PORK WITH SCRAMBLED EGGS**

Hot spiced chicken along with a hot steamed white rice.

## INGREDIENTS: 4 servings

| | |
|---|---|
| ¹/₂ C | sliced forest mushrooms |
| ¹/₂ C | tiger lily buds |
| ¹/₄ C | cloud ears |
| ¹/₂ C | bamboo shoots, sliced |
| 3 | eggs |
| ¹/₂ t | salt |
| 1 T | oil |
| 2 T | oil |
| ¹/₂ lb (225 g) | boneless pork, sliced thin |
| 2 T | *mirin* |
| Dash | soy sauce |
| ¹/₄ C | soup stock |
| 2 | green onions, chopped |
| 1 | head lettuce |

\* For a spicy taste, add 1 t of hot bean paste.
\* Use carrots for added color.

Separate the head of lettuce, using small leaves as cups, and place on a platter.

1. Soak mushrooms, tiger lily buds; and cloud ears until soft (10 min). Wash well and slice thin. Set aside.

2. Beat eggs, adding salt. Fry in 1 T oil in the wok to make scrambled eggs and set aside.

3. Add 2 T oil to wok and cook pork on high heat 2 or 3 min.

4. Add mushrooms, tiger lily buds, cloud ears, bamboo shoots, carrots, *mirin* and soy sauce. Stir together, adding soup stock, cover, bring to boil and cook 1 min.

5. Add green onions and mix in eggs, breaking into small pieces. Serve with lettuce cup, steamed white rice or MANDARIN PANCAKES (pg. 46).

**PRESENTATION**

**Serve with FRIED RICE (p. 38).**

## INGREDIENTS: 4 servings

| | |
|---|---|
| ½ C | cooked meat (chicken, pork, shrimp, or crab) |
| ½ C | bamboo shoots |
| ½ C | onions |
| 1 | stalk celery (½ C) |
| 1 C | bean sprouts |
| 3 | large eggs |
| 1 t | salt |
| ¼ C | oil for frying |

Chopped green onions and toasted sesame seeds for garnish

**Gravy**

| | |
|---|---|
| 1¼ C | cold soup stock |
| 2 T | cornstarch |
| 1 T | *mirin* |
| 1 T | soy sauce |

Bring gravy to a full boil, stirring constantly, just before serving.

∗ Patties may be made ahead and reheated in the oven. Place on cookie sheet and bake at 375°F (190°C) for 5 min.

1. Chop meat, bamboo shoots, onions and celery. Do not chop the bean sprouts.

2. Beat eggs with the salt and add to the filling ingredients just before frying.

3. Heat an electric or frying pan to 375°F (190°C). Pour in the ¼ C oil.

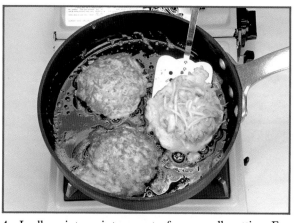

4. Ladle mixture into pan to form small patties. Fry about 2 min, turn over and fry 3 min more. Adjust temperature as needed (6-8 patties). Wipe pan clean and repeat process, using more oil as needed, until all patties are fried.

5. Serve with hot gravy. Garnish with chopped green onions and toasted sesame seeds.

**PRESENTATION**

# 釀豆腐 DEEP-FRIED STUFFED *TOFU*

Serve with a chicken dish.

## INGREDIENTS: 4 servings

| | | | |
|---|---|---|---|
| 1 | cube of *tofu* (bean curd), 1 lb (450g) | 1 T | oil |
| **Filling** | | 1 | clove garlic, minced |
| 1/3 C | ground pork | 2 | forest mushrooms (soaked, rinsed and sliced) |
| 1/3 C | chopped prawns (shelled, deveined) | | |
| 1 T | chopped water chestnuts | 1/4 t | salt |
| 1 | forest mushroom chopped (soaked and rinsed) | 1 T | soy sauce or oyster sauce |
| | | 1 t | rice wine |
| 1/4 t | salt | 1 C | soup stock |
| 1 t | rice wine | | |
| 1 t | soy sauce | 3 C | lettuce or celery cabbage, sliced |
| 1 t | sesame seed oil | 1 | green onion, chopped |
| 1 T | cornstarch | 1 t | sesame seed oil |
| | | Some cornstarch for thickening | |
| 3 C | oil (350°F, 175°C) | | |

1. Drain *tofu* (bean curd) well.

2. Combine ingredients of filling.

3. Cut the 1 lb (450 g) cube of *tofu* (bean curd) into 4 equal pieces. Cut each piece diagonally in half, forming a triangle. With a sharp knife, gently remove some of the *tofu*, forming a pocket in each triangle.

4. Carefully stuff each triangle with about 1 T filling.

5. Heat 3 C oil in the wok to 350°F (175°C). Deep-fry several triangles at a time until light brown (5 min), turning once. Remove and set aside. Repeat with the other pieces.

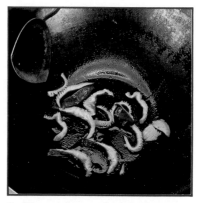

6. Heat a clean wok or frying pan; add 1 T oil and fry garlic for a few seconds. Add mushrooms, salt, soy sauce, wine, soup stock.

7. Add stuffed triangles. Cover, bring to a boil, reduce temperature and simmer for 5 min.

8. Turn temperature up to high, add lettuce and cook until wilted. Add green onions and sesame seed oil. Thicken with cornstarch and water. To serve: Place lettuce on bottom of dish and triangles on top.

**PRESENTATION**

## Serve with ALMOND BREADED CHICKEN (p. 54).

### INGREDIENTS: 4 servings

| | |
|---|---|
| 1 | cube of *tofu* (bean curd), 1 lb (450 g) |
| 1 T | oil |
| 1 | clove garlic, minced |
| 1/2 C | ground pork |
| 2 t | hot bean paste (or to taste) |
| 1 T | soy sauce |
| 1/4 t | salt |
| 3/4 C | soup stock |

| | |
|---|---|
| Some | cornstarch and water for thickening |
| 1 | green onion, chopped |
| 1 t | sesame seed oil |

✳ To give the *tofu* a firmer texture, cut *tofu* into 1 in (2 1/2 cm) cubes. Fry cubes in an oiled non-stick frying pan to lightly brown all sides.

1. Cut *tofu* (bean curd) into 1/2 in (1 1/2 cm) cubs. Set aside.

2. Heat wok, add oil, garlic and ground pork. Stir-fry pork on high heat until done (2 min). Add hot bean paste, soy sauce, salt, soup stock and *tofu*.

3. Cover, bring to a boil and cook gently for 2 min. Thicken with cornstarch mixture to desired thickness. Add green onions and sesame seed oil. Mix gently to combine all ingredients.

**PRESENTATION**

# Information

This section provides a working knowledge of the basic cutting and cooking techniques, menu planning and helpful tips necessary in the preparation of a successful and delicious Chinese meal.

# CUTTING METHODS

In Chinese cooking, all ingredients are cut into bite-size morsels before cooking or serving. This is done for aesthetic as well as functional reasons. Vegetables are more appealing with uniform slicing and chopping while ingredients cut the same size and shape cook more evenly and quickly. The following describes the various cutting techniques used in this book.

- **Slice** — Refers to meats or vegetables cut into thin uniform strips usually two inches long by ¾ to 1 in (2 to 2½ cm) wide and about ⅛ in (½ cm) thick or as directed by the recipe.
- **Sliver or Shred** — Refers to meats or vegetables cut 2 in (5 cm) long by ⅛ in (½ cm) wide by ⅛ in (½ cm) thick to resemble match-sticks or beansprouts.
- **Dice** — To cut into ½ in (1½ cm) cubes.
- **Chop or Mince** — To cut into small pieces as in ground beef.

## • Boning a chicken

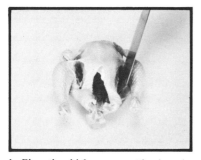

1. Place the chicken on a cutting board, breast side up. With a sharp knife, slice through the skin between the thigh and lower breast, exposing the thigh.

2. Bend the thigh back and carve around the joint to remove the thigh and leg. Remove as much meat as possible from the back of the chicken while removing the thigh and leg. Repeat with the other side in the same manner.

3. To remove meat from leg and thigh: Cut along the inside of the leg and thigh, exposing the bones. Cut the meat away from the thigh bone, separate the joint, and remove the thigh bone. Remove the rest of the meat from the leg bone. Repeat with the other leg and thigh.

4. Turn chicken over so the back is up. Cut the wings from the back to expose the joint, taking as much meat as possible from the back. Separate at the joint and pull to remove breast meat. This will leave a small piece of chicken (tenderloin) still attached to the breast bone, which should be cut out. Repeat with the other wing in the same manner.

5. Trim off as much meat from the carcass as possible. Use the bones to make soup stock.

# CUTTING METHODS

## •How to bone a chicken breast

1. Place chicken breast skin side down on a cutting board. Cut ½ in (1½cm) into the top of the chicken breast, breaking the white triangular piece of cartilage.

2. Holding the chicken breast with both hands, bend it back to expose the breast bone. The bone should pop up.

3. Run thumb down the breast bone and cartilage.

4. Pull the entire bone and cartilage out.

5. Locate the wishbone at the top of the breast, which broke into two pieces when the breast was bent back. Using a sharp knife, cut as much meat from the wishbone as possible.

6. Release meat from the ribs, scraping the bones as you cut. Repeat with the other side of the chicken breast.

7. Pull skin off and cut off the fat at the bottom of the breast.

8. Remove the tendons on the underside of the breast. There is one on each side. Now you have a boneless chicken breast. Use as directed in a recipe.

## •Carving a chicken

1. Remove wings, legs and thighs, set aside.
2. Separate breast from the back; set breast aside.
3. First, cut the back into bite-sized pieces (1½ × 2 in, 4 × 5 cm) and arrange on the center of a platter.
4. Separate wings at the joints, discard tips and place wing pieces on the sides of the upper half of the platter.
5. Cut each thigh in half and place on platter. Place the legs on the sides of the lower half of the platter.
6. Cut breast into bite-sized pieces and place on top of back pieces.
7. Garnish with parsley.

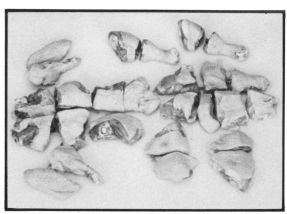

This method of carving can also be used to cut a chicken in preparation for cooking.

# COOKING METHODS

The most common Chinese cooking methods include stir-frying, deep-frying, roasting, and steaming. Depending upon the method utilized, ingredients generally retain their natural flavor and nutrition with new and different tastes emerging from the use of each method.

## • Stir-Frying

This method of cooking combines the elements of high heat and quick, constant tossing to seal in the flavor and juices of meats and vegetables. Stir-frying cooks protein foods thoroughly at the same time leaving them tender and juicy. Vegetables stir-fried until barely tender retain their natural color and crisp texture.

Only a small amount of oil is necessary. Timing and temperature will vary according to the type of pan selected and whether a gas or electric range is used. A flat-bottomed pan or wok which has contact with the heating element will get much hotter than a round-bottomed one. In addition, a gas range is more convenient since you can turn the heat up or down instantly. A good stir-frying temperature is 375°F (190°C). If the temperature is too high, the food will burn in which case a lower temperature adjustment is in order. On the other hand, if the temperature is too low, ingredients do not fry, but seep in the oil and will lose their flavor. Therefore, to maintain the proper temperature, constant adjustment of the temperature may be necessary.

Actual stir-frying involves vigorous arm action in the constant stirring and tossing of the food. It is a loud and noisy operation when the food meets the pan and the stirring begins. Actual cooking time will seldom exceed several minutes.

**Follow the steps below for effective stir-frying:**

1) Heat the wok until it barely gets hot and add oil (usually 2 T).
2) Roll the oil around to cover the cooking surface of the wok.
3) When the oil begins to form a light haze, you are ready to add the ingredients.
4) Follow the recipe and remember to adjust the temperature control for the proper stir-frying temperature.

## • Cornstarch for Thickening

Sauces or gravies can be thickened with a variety of starches such as arrowroot, potato, tapioca, or cornstarch. All of these starches produce a translucent gravy, whereas flour will produce an opaque gravy. In Chinese cooking, cornstarch is most often used.

Many recipes call for cornstarch for thickening, but sometimes an exact amount is not given. Mix equal amounts of cornstarch to cold water and stir until cornstarch is dissolved. Usually 1 T cornstarch dissolved in 1 T cold water will be enough to thicken $1/2$ C sauce to produce a medium thick gravy.

To thicken a sauce, always push all ingredients to the side of the wok, making a well at the bottom of the wok. Stir cornstarch mixture and pour a small amount into the well. Stir the sauce constantly to prevent lumps. Allow the sauce to come to a boil and see how thick it is. If not thick enough, add more cornstarch mixture until desired thickness is obtained. Always remember to stir the sauce constantly to prevent lumps from forming. When desired thickness is obtained, mix ingredients together gently to coat with sauce.

## • Deep-Frying

Deep-frying requires a large amount of oil in the wok, usually not more than 3-4 C. A 14 in (35 cm) wok is best suited for deep-frying. As with stir-frying, timing and temperature for deep-frying will vary depending upon whether a gas or electric stove is used. Thus, the time given for most recipes is only approximate and adjustments should be made accordingly. Added caution should be exercised whenever oil is used at high temperatures. Never leave the hot oil unattended!

The proper temperature for deep-frying is generally 375°F (190°C). The oil should reach this temperature before any ingredients are added. At a temperature of 375°F (190°C) the oil will just barely begin to smoke. An easy way to tell whether the oil has reached the desired temperature is to add a drop of batter into the oil. If the drop of batter sinks and slowly returns to the surface, the oil is not yet hot enough. If the batter drops to the bottom and immediately bounces up to the surface, the oil is ready for deep-frying. If the oil smokes, it has gotten too hot and the temperature should be lowered.

The oil used for deep-frying can be saved and used again. To grant your oil longer life, remove food

# COOKING METHODS

crumbs with the fine mesh strainer during deep-frying. The quality of used oil is judged by its clarity, not by the number of times used nor the length of time used. Fresh oil is light yellow in color and clear. If the used oil is still relatively clear, it is salvageable and readily usable again. However, used oil which appears darker and clouded should be discarded because the temperature at which it will begin to smoke will drop and consequently, a high enough temperature cannot be achieved for proper deep-frying resulting in foods turning out very greasy.

To store the used oil, first strain with a fine mesh strainer. Then place the oil in a heatproof container if the oil is still hot. Allow the oil to cool, cover, and store in the refrigerator until ready to use again. Peanut oil or good vegetable oil such as corn oil will have a longer usable life as well as possess qualities superior to other oils for purposes of deep-frying foods. None of the pure vegetable oils contain cholesterol and the use of a polyunsaturated oil is strongly recommended.

**Follow the steps below for effective deep-frying:**
1) Heat 3-4 C oil in the wok until a light haze forms at approximately 375°F (190°C).
2) Drop in foods and deep-fry until foods are cooked.
3) Adjust the temperature to maintain a constant frying temperature of 375°F (190°C). Begin by setting temperature on high; if the oil gets too hot (smokes), turn down temperature to medium high and back to high if the oil drops below 375°F (190°C).
4) Follow the instructions given in the recipe.

## •Roasting, Baking, or Broiling

These cooking methods are so common and ordinary as to require limited explanation.

Meats or rolls may be roasted or baked in the oven. When roasting meats, use a broiling pan or place a rack on the bottom of a pan to support the meat. Add a small amount of water to the bottom of the pan, making sure the meat is above the water level. The water will keep the meat moist and also keep the drippings from burning onto the broiling pan.

**Follow the steps below for effective roasting, baking or broiling:**
1) Preheat the oven to the required temperature.
2) Place all foods in the center of the oven to allow for even roasting.
3) Follow the instructions given in the recipe.

## •Steaming

Steaming is one of the most nutritious, not to mention convenient, methods of cooking foods, retaining more nutrients and natural flavor than other conventional means of cooking. Steamed foods seal in natural juices of meats and vegetables which are delicious served over rice.

There are many different types of steamers available. The wok with a cover will serve as a good steamer. Multi-tiered bamboo steamers may be purchased. However, a large pot with a cover will suffice for the purpose of steaming food.

Steaming racks are required to support and elevate the plate or bowl which contains food to be steamed in a wok. A round cake rack will serve just as well as commercially available steaming racks. You may even improvise, using a water chestnut can with both ends removed as a substitue for a steaming rack. The rack should be sent in the center of the wok or pan.

All steamers operate according to the same basic principle. The efficient circulation of steam is of paramount importance. Bamboo steamers have several tiers in which many dishes can be steamed simultaneously. The tiers and cover are set on top of a wok containing boiling water. There are also metal steamers consisting of a pot to hold the water and usually two tiers and a cover. For example, the bottom pot functions to cook soup stock while the two tiers are used to steam two other separate dishes. In this manner, many dishes may be steamed at one time saving both time and energy.

**Follow the steps below for effective steaming:**
1) Pour water in the wok or pot so that the water level stands one inch below the steaming rack or dish of food.
2) Cover the wok and bring the water to a full boil.
3) Use heatproof dishes only for steaming.
4) Insert the dish of food atop the steaming rack. Cover and bring to full boil (or full steam) again. Turn the temperature down to medium high and allow to steam for the specified time.
5) Check the water level when longer steaming times are necessary.

# MENU PLANNING

In serving a Chinese meal, there is no single main course as in the typical American meal, but a combination of courses to be presented simultaneously for everyone to enjoy. The Chinese serve two different types of meals depending upon the occasion and circumstances. The formal banquet dinner is appropriate for a larger group of people celebrating a special event while the more common informal dinner is more of a practical everyday meal. The recipes and emphasis of this book are directed toward the successful preparation of an informal Chinese meal and I would strongly suggest mastering the preparation of an informal dinner before attempting to serve a banquet.

A formal Chinese banquet is served to a gathering of ten or more guests customarily seated around a large round table with a revolving "Lazy Susan" in the center of the table for easy access to individual dinner courses by the guests. The banquet would normally consist of ten courses served in a particular order by a staff of servants. A large platter of cold meat and vegetable appetizers is usually first to arrive. Then follows two to four stir-fried dishes. The banquet always includes a hot soup which may be served at any point in the banquet, but traditionally near the end of the meal. The premier entrees such as a whole duck or fish would follow the stir-fried dishes. Rice or noodles would then be served to complete the banquet. All the dishes are brought out in quick succession to insure that all courses are hot and delicious. Finally, tea is served to end the banquet. Wine may also be served throughout the entire meal. The Chinese banquet is very elaborate and as such, should be reserved for very special occasions.

The informal Chinese dinner is more appropriately suited for the life styles of today. Nutritious, economical, and easy to prepare, Chinese food is most of all delicious. Therefore, I have devoted this book to the preparation of dishes used in an everyday Chinese meal. The informal dinner is designed for a party of four people. In any event, keep the group to less than ten people unless you plan to serve a buffet style dinner.

Planning your menu is the important first step in preparing the meal. Always prepare as much in advance as possible so as to be able to enjoy your company instead of being stuck in the kitchen. It is also a good practice to try a recipe before cooking it for guests. Always read the entire recipe before starting to cook.

# MENU PLANNING

## MENU CHART

| Number of People Served: | 2 | 4 | 6 | 8 | 10 |
|---|---|---|---|---|---|
| **Course** | | | | | |
| **APPETIZER** | * | * | * | * | * |
| **SOUP** | * | * | * | * | * |
| **RICE** | * | * | * | * | * |
| (Allow $\frac{1}{2}$ Cup uncooked or $1\frac{1}{2}$ Cups cooked rice per person) | | | | | |
| -BEEF | 1 | 1 | 1 | 1 | 1 |
| **MEAT**-CHICKEN | | | 1 | 1 | 1 |
| -PORK | | | | 1 | 1 |
| (Selection of beef, chicken, or pork dish is up to you) | | | | | |
| **SEAFOOD** | | 1 | 1 | 1 | 1 |
| **VEGETABLE** | 1 | 1 | $1\frac{1}{2}$ | 2 | $2\frac{1}{2}$ or 3 |
| **DESSERT** | * | * | * | * | * |
| (Usually fresh fruit) | | | | | |

\* ADJUST RECIPE FOR NUMBER OF PEOPLE.

The above menu chart illustrates sample menus for varying groups of people. For instance, an informal meal for four people would consist of one each of an appetizer, soup, rice or noodle, meat of your choice, seafood, and vegetable dish.

Generally, rice always accompanies a Chinese meal. Dessert is usually fresh fruit in season and tea is served at the end of the meal.

For every two additional people, i.e., 6, 8, 10, add one meat dish of your choice and increase the vegetable selection by $\frac{1}{2}$ recipe. Rather than increase the recipe, you may prefer to make two different vegetable dishes. When in doubt as to how much food to prepare, remember it is far better to have leftovers than to run short of food at the dinner table.

When planning your menu, always consider the balance of flavors, the required ingredients, and cutting/cooking methods previously mentioned. Incorporate different meats and vegetables to vary the menu. For example, cook one dish of chicken, one dish of beef, and one dish of pork instead of three chicken dishes.

However, you may also economize by working the menu around one major roast or meat. By using a pork loin end roast for instance, portions of the roast can be cut for barbecued pork or sweet and sour pork. Bits and pieces of pork may further be used in the making of won ton filling or chow mein. The remaining bones may then be simmered for an excellent soup stock. Even the last bits of cooked pork on the bones can be removed and used in fried rice or egg fu yung. This efficient and economical use of meat also applies to the use of a whole chicken. Whenever possible, balance the menu by serving a different meat dish or use different meats in the vegetable dishes. You can always save what is not used for another meal with the aid of a freezer to preserve your meats.

The greatest assets in Chinese cooking are your resourcefulness, ingenuity, and ability to adapt in the face of unavailable ingredients. Shopping for weekly specials at your grocery store and preparing your menu accordingly will save you money. Of course, you may always choose to increase a recipe rather than prepare two separate recipes which will necessitate a shorter list of required ingredients.

**An informal Chinese dinner is served with all the different courses placed at the center of the table simultaneously and everyone helps themselves.**

An individual place setting is illustrated below.

1. Individual Plate—A luncheon or medium size plate to accommodated individual servings of food
2. Individual Rice Bowl—A bowl used for soup initially and then used to hold rice. Two separate bowls may be used instead.
3. Small Plate—A dish used to hold soy sauce or dips.
4. Soup Spoon
5. Chopsticks—Bamboo, wood, or ivory utensils used for picking up food and eating.
6. Tea cup—A small porcelain cup used for serving tea at the end of meal.

## • Seating Arrangement

The seating arrangement is only important in serving a formal Chinese banquet. The guest of honor is seated at the head of the table which is situated furthest from the serving door while the host and/or hostess sits directly opposite facing the guest. People usually sit in any order they choose while participating in an informal Chinese dinner.

## • Order of Service

The various courses of food should arrive at the table at nearly the same time and placed in the center of the table. Dishes are passed around and everyone serves themselves using either serving spoons or chopsticks. The particular order in which food courses are served in a formal Chinese banquet as earlier explained need not be adhered to in an informal Chinese dinner.

## • Beverages

The common beverages which accompany a Chinese meal are wine and tea. However, soup is also considered a beverage in a Chinese dinner. Soup is consumed throughout the meal. But for convenience in serving and minimizing dirty dishes, the Western custom of serving soup first may be followed. The same bowl may be used for soup, and then used for rice.

## • Wine

Wine served with a Chinese meal is a mere accompaniment to the diversity of flavors in Chinese foods. Shaohsing wine, a rice wine, served warm in porcelain cups, is the most popular wine. However, with so many good Western and European wines to select from, serve what appeals to the palates of you and your guests.

## • Tea

Tea is the traditional drink served immediately before and after a Chinese meal. The choice of tea is entirely up to individual tastes. There are basically three groups of teas.

Green tea—unfermented, dried in the sun. Delicate flavor and is light in color.
Oolong tea—partially fermented green tea imparting a slightly stronger flavor.
Red or Black tea—fermented teas which are first dried in the sun and then fired over charcoal. They possess the strongest flavor among the three varieties of tea.
The scented teas of which jasmine tea is by far the most popular, are made mostly from partially fermented tea.
Tea is properly brewed in porcelain pots and cups. Clean and heat the teapot by pouring in brisk boiling water and waiting until the teapot is warm before discarding the water. Next, add tea leaves and pour in fresh boiling water. Allow the covered tea to steep for approximately three minutes. The tea leaves may be reused for a second or even third brewing, but remember to leave some tea in the pot for the next brewing in order for the tea to release its full aroma.

# BASIC EQUIPMENT

### Wok

The Chinese wok is a round or flat-bottomed pan made of heavy gauge carbon steel. It comes in various sizes, but the most functional for our purposes is the 14in (35cm) wok. The round-bottomed wok is usually accompanied by a ventilated ring which serves to support the base of the wok above a gas-range burner. A flat-bottomed wok, which does not require a ring stand, sits atop an electric range, but requires some adjustments during cooking as there is direct contact with the burner, resulting in much hotter temperatures.

When using a gas range, the ring should be situated with the sides slanting downwards and the smaller opening supporting the wok. The round-buttom design of the wok directs the heat source to the center of the wok which gets hot very quickly. The heat is then conducted rapidly and evenly throughout the rest of the wok. When using an electric range, the ring should be placed securely over the burner, with the sides slanting upwards to allow the center of the wok closer proximity to the burner.

#### Seasoning wok

Scrub the wok in hot sudsy water to remove the protective oil applied when manufactured. Rinse well and dry thoroughly. Season the cleaned wok by heating and rubbing a small amount of peanut oil on the inside surface with a paper towel. Re-heat the wok until hot and repeat the process two more times. Your wok is now ready for use.

During the course of cooking a meal, the wok need only be cleaned with hot water, using a bristle scrub brush used for Teflon pans. When you are through using the wok, wash in sudsy water and rinse. Dry over medium heat and rub a dab of oil on the inside surface to prevent rust. Eventually, with constant use, your wok will assume a darker color on the inside which results in smooth non-stick cooking. Never scour your wok with harsh cleansers. If rust appears, simply scrub clean and reseason. Any time the wok is used for steaming, it must be reseasoned afterward in order to prevent foods from sticking. However, only one coating of oil is necessary for reseasoning your wok.

Electric woks are good substitutes. They are espeically suited for entertaining or cooking at the table. Just follow the package instructions for use and care.

### Wok Accessorles

Accessories specially designed for wok cooking are available in any cookware store. They greatly facilitate cooking with a wok.

**Cover** — This size of the dome-shaped cover depends largely upon the diameter of the wok. Sometimes a 10-12in (25-30cm) cover to a frying pan may suffice. The convenience of a cover is readily apparent when it is necessary to steam ingredients using the wok.

**Curved Spatula** — This utensil comes with a long handle with a wide, curved edge which fits the curved bottom of the wok. Ingredients can be more readily tossed and removed using a curved rather than straight-edged spatula.

**Draining Rack** — This wire semicircular rack attaches to the top of the wok. It is used in deep-frying to drain the oil from the food before removing onto a serving dish.

**Wire Strainer** — This strainer is made of wire with a long wooden handle. The large holes allow the ingredients to be removed quickly from hot oil, leaving the crumbs or bits of batter behind to be removed by a fine mesh strainer. It is also useful in removing large pieces of foods from soups or sauces.

**Fine Mesh Strainer** — This wire utensil is used in deep-frying to remove small particles of food, thereby keeping the oil clean. It can also be used to strain bits of food from soup stock.

**Steaming Rack** — This round rack, preferably made of metal, resembles a cake rack. It is used to elevate plates of food above the boiling water in a wok while steaming. Bamboo or metal steamers with two tiers and a cover are also available, but unless a lot of food is steamed, a wok and steaming rack is sufficient.

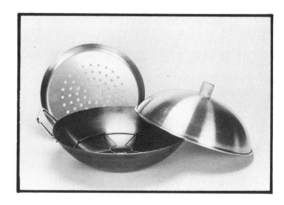

**Deep-Frying Thermometer** — This handy device will ensure the exact oil temperature used in recipes calling for deep-frying.

**Cooking Chopsticks** — These are longer than ordinary eating chopsticks. They are made of bamboo and come in various lengths. Choose the proper length by the comfort and ease of handling best suited to you.

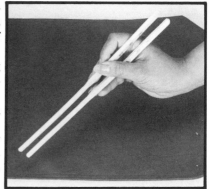

How to use 1) Rest the first chopstick on top of your ring finger with the thumb braced over the chopstick.

2) Hold the other chopstick as you would a pencil.

3) With the inside chopstick held stationary with your thumb, move the outside chopstick, forming pinchers to pick up ingredients.

## Cleaver

The basic Chinese knife is the cleaver. It is used for cutting recipe ingredients and in the same motion, transporting them to an awaiting wok or serving tray. The cleaver usually measures 3-4 in (8-10 cm) wide and 8 in (20 cm) long. The thickness varies from thin cleavers for vegetable slicing all the way to thick bone-chopping cleavers. A sharp cleaver is necessary to perform the various cutting methods discussed in the next section. Keep your cleaver sharp by using a sharpening stone and steel as often as needed.

## Rice Cooker

This is a very useful item if you cook rice often or when a large quantity of steamed rice is desired. The electric rice cooker automatically steams the rice to the proper consistency and keeps it warm until ready to serve. Rice cookers come in various capacities.

This is the basic equipment designed for Chinese cooking. Always keep in mind that alternatives in your own kitchen may work just as well. Many ordinary kitchen utensils can be adapted for use in Chinese cooking. Substitutes for the basic equipment range from a heavy frying pan in place of the traditional Chinese wok all the way to miscellaneous knives for the cleaver.

# GLOSSARY

**Anise, star**

Brown, star shaped seed with the taste of licorice. Used as a spice for sauces. Keeps indefinitely on shelf.

**Bamboo shoot**

Cream colored, cone shaped shoots of bamboo. Canned shoots are most common. Once opened, store covered with fresh water up to 2 weeks in the refrigerator. Change water once every 4 to 5 days.

**Bean curd, fermented (fu yu)**

Fermented white bean curd with a cheesy flavor. It is sold bottled in half inch thick squares. Keeps in refrigerator indefinitely after opening.

**Bean curd, fresh (*tofu*)**

Usually square shaped, creamy textured, bland curd made from soybeans. Also comes deep-fried and canned. Fresh bean curd, covered with water, can be kept in the refrigerator for approximately one week. Remove from original package and replace with fresh water as soon as possible. Change water every 2 days to keep fresh.

**Bean curd, red (nam yu)**

Sometimes called wet bean curd. Red soft cubes of fermented bean curd with a strong cheesy flavor. Comes in cans. Once opened, store in jars with a tight lid in the refrigerator indefinitely.

**Bean filling, sweet**

Thick, sweet bean paste made from beans and sugar. Often used as a filling for pastries. Usually sold in cans. Store tightly covered in refrigerator or freezer indefinitely.

**Bean sauce, brown or yellow**

Sauce made from soybeans and salt. Often comes in cans. Some bean sauces may contain bean halves and others may be a smooth sauce, similar to Japanese red *miso*, which can be used as a substitute in some recipes. Keeps indefinitely in the refrigerator in a tightly sealed jar.

**Bean threads (salfun or cellophane noodles)**

Thin, long, dry noodles made of mung bean flour. Keeps on shelf indefinitely. Soak in warm water for 15 min before use. May also be deep-fried in hot oil. Do not soak in water if used for deep-frying. Use as a noodle in soups or with stir fried vegetables and meats. To keep clean up to a minimum, place noodles in a large paper bag before removing wrapper. Break off amount needed and store remainder in bag.

**Bean paste, hot (chili paste with soybean)**

Soybean sauce made from soybeans, chili peppers and sometimes garlic. Comes in cans or jars. Refrigerated, keeps indefinitely in tightly sealed jars. Degree of hotness may vary between different brands. Brown soybean sauce combined with a hot sauce can be used as a substitute.

**Bean sprouts**

Sprouts of the mung bean; about 2 in (5 cm) long. Refrigerate sprouts covered with water. Keeps for one week. Change the water every 3 days.

**Bitter melon**

Long, green, pear-shaped melon with a ridged surface. It has a definite bitter taste. Cut melon in half lengthwise and remove seeds. Cut in thin slices and stir-fry with meats.

**Black beans, fermented**

Salted, fermented, soft black bean seed. Mainly used to flavor sauces. Rinse with water before using. Keeps in a covered container on the shelf indefinitely.

**Bok choy (Chinese cabbage or greens)**

Dark green leafy vegetable with a white stalk. Keeps in refrigerator for one week. High in vitamins A and C.

**Broccoli, Chinese**

A tender, green, seasonal vegetable available in spring and summer months. Chinese broccoli is more slender and leafy than regular broccoli. For recipes in this book, substitute with bok choy, spinach or regular broccoli cut into long slender pieces.

**Cleaver**

The knife used to do most all cutting in Chinese cooking. Usually a lighter, thinner cleaver is used for slicing and chopping meats and vegetables. The heavier cleaver is used to cut through bone.

### Cloud ears

Brown, irregular, leafy shaped fungus or mushroom with a delicate taste. Soak 15 min in warm water to soften. Rinse before using. Keeps indefinitely on shelf when dried. Also called tree ears.

### Five spice

Blend of five ground spices; Szechuan peppercorns, star anise, cinnamon, fennel and cloves. Keeps on shelf for several months.

### Ginger root

Irregular bulb root of the ginger plant. Hot and spicy in taste. Slice ginger and freeze separated slices. Keeps in the freezer indefinitely. Peel ginger and store in rice wine. Slice and use as needed.

### Harly melon (jit gwa)

Oval shaped, green melon with a hairy surface. Peel, slice thin and use in soup.

### Hoisin sauce

Pungent, sweet condiment sauce made of soybeans, spices, chili and sugar. Once opened, store in a jar with tight lid. Keeps refrigerated for about 6 months.

### Jelly fish

Body of the jelly fish cut into shreds. Usually sold salted and packaged in plastic bags in the refrigerator section. Store in refrigerator or freezer. Rinse off salt and soak in cold water before using.

### Litchi nuts

A sweet, white fruit about 1 in (2½ cm) in diameter. It has a dark red hull which must be removed before eating. Also comes canned and dried. Use as a garnish or as a fruit.

### Long beans, Chinese

Foot long, thin green beans. When cooked, resemble string beans but have a more delicate flavor. Treat in same manner as regular green beans.

### Maifun (rice noodles)

Noodles made from rice flour. Soak until soft in hot water before using. Also, noodles may be deep-fried in hot oil. Do not soak before deep-frying. To keep clean up to a minimum, place package of noodles in a large paper bag before removing wrapper. Break off amounts as needed. Store remainder in the bag.

### *Mirin*

Japanese sweet rice wine used in cooking to bring out flavor or to add a little sweetness. Not interchangeable with rice wine.

### *Miso*

Fermented bean paste made from soybeans and rice. Used mainly in Japanese cooking. Red or *aka miso* is saltier and white or *shiro miso* is milder or sweeter. Red *miso* is a good substitute for brown bean sauce. Refrigerator *miso* in sealed containers indefinitely.

### Mushroom, dried (forest or black)

Dried black forest mushrooms have a delicate flavor. Can be stored in covered container on the shelf, indefinitely. Must soak in warm water until soft, rinse, discard stem and use in recipe.

### Mustard, dried

Pungent powder. When mixed with water, forms sauce which is used as a dip to accompany barbecued pork and other foods. Store dry powder on shelf indefinitely. Mix 1 T water to 1 T dry powder for average proportion.

### Oyster sauce

Thick brown sauce made from oysters and soy sauce. Used to enhance flavor or as a dip. Keeps indefinitely in the refrigerator.

### Panko (dehydrated bread crumbs)

Japanese dehydrated bread crumbs with a coarser texture than regular bread crumbs. Available at most supermarkets or oriental groceries. To make panko, use white bread and make coarse crumbs in the blender. Then dry crumbs slightly in the oven.

### Parsley, Chinese (corlander or cilantro)

A leafy parsley with a pungent flavor. Use as a garnish. Also may be used to add flavor to most any dish

### Sausage, Chinese (lop cheong)

Cured pork sausages about 6 in (15 cm) in length with a sweet flavor. Refrigerate up to one month or freeze up to several months.

### Seaweed, dried

Dried seaweed is usually available in sheets. Keeps indefinitely on the shelf. Some seaweed sheets are more expensive because they are roasted and seasoned. These are used in Japanese cooking.

## Sesame seed oil
Golden brown oil of sesame seeds. Buy in small quantities and keep refrigerated after opening. Add to dishes just before serving.

## Shrimp, dried
Dried tiny shrimp. Soak in warm water for about $1/2$ hour to soften before use. Keeps on shelf indefinitely in covered jars.

## Snow peas (Chinese pea pods)
Flat edible pea pod. Has a delicate taste and comes fresh or frozen. Must string as in green beans before cooking.

## Soy sauce
The extract of fermented soybeans combined with salt. Soy sauce range from light to dark. Light soy sauce is the most delicate, and is used as a dip or in cooking; gives little color. Some dark soy sauce has caramel added for color and is slightly sweet. Japanese soy sauce is in the middle and serves most purposes very well. For most recipes, Kikkoman soy sauce may be used unless specified differently in recipe.

## Stir-fry
To toss, cook or saute in English, chow in Chinese. Slices of vegetables, meats, or a combination are cooked quickly in the wok with a small amount of oil. Liquid may be added to make a sauce and cornstarch is used for thickening. Foods retain more food value, color and texture.

## Szechuan vegetable
The knobby bulb of a radish preserved in chili pepper and salt. Rinse before using. Store air-tight in jar. Refrigerate indefinitely. No substitutes.

## Tiger lily flowers
Dried golden brown tiger lily flowers; about 2 in (5 cm) long. Soak in warm water about 15 min and rinse before use. Keeps indefinitely on shelf when dry.

## Turnip, Chinese (lo bok or daikon)
Crisp large white root vegetable resembling a large carrot. Peel skin and slice or shred before cooking. Store in the refrigerator.

## Vinegar, rice
A mild vinegar made from rice. Used in most oriental dishes. Keeps indefinitely on the shelf.

## Water chestnuts
Walnut sized, brown bulb. Must be peeled before use. It is sweet and has a crisp texture similar to apples. Canned water chestnuts are peeled and boiled. They will keep covered with fresh water, in the refrigerator, for about 2 weeks. Change the water once a week.

## Wine lees
A thick fermented wine paste. Light *miso* (Japanese soybean paste) can be used as a substitute.

## Wine, Shaohsing or rice
Chinese rice wine used for drinking or cooking. Dry sherry may be used as a substitute in cooking.

## Winter melon (tung gwa)
A large light green melon with a white powdery surface resembling a water melon. The inside is white with seeds in the center. Usually sold in sections. Peel hard skin and discard seeds. Slice melon and use in soups.

## Wok
The wok is a metal pan with sloping sides and a rounded or flat bottom. The 14 in (35 cm) wok is the best size for home use. Refer to wok in the information section of this book.

## Won tons
Fresh squares of noodle dough. Usually comes in one pound packages. Thickness varies from thick to thin. Fresh won tons will keep in the refrigerator one week. Can be frozen, wrapped air tight, for about 2 months. Use thick wrappers for deep-fried won tons. Thin wrappers are better for soups

# INDEX